For my beloved [...]

The queeniest of [...]   ...sM,

The rosiest of tra[...]   , PERVERSION,

The most dignified of divas,   AND THE

Thank you for all your   MASTERY OF

support & "performativity."   DESIRE

Love,

Kevin

"Beethoven Kissing Lizst."
Lithograph from "Erin-
nerung an das 5ojährige
Jubiläum des Franz Lizst,"
1873. Budapest, Lizst
Memorial Hall.

KEVIN KOPELSON

Beethoven's Kiss

*Pianism, Perversion, and
the Mastery of Desire*

Stanford University Press
Stanford, California

Stanford University Press,
Stanford, California
© 1996 by the Board of Trustees of the
Leland Stanford Junior University
Printed in the United States of America

CIP data appear at the end of the book

Stanford University Press publications
are distributed exclusively by
Stanford University Press within the
United States, Canada, Mexico,
and Central America; they are distributed
exclusively by Cambridge
University Press throughout the rest
of the world.

FOR

∽ *Linda Dunn Turchin*
1935-1976

Acknowledgments

I began my first book as a doctoral dissertation at Brown University. I began this one as a love letter to Wayne Koestenbaum. It still is, of course. But like any such letter, *Beethoven's Kiss* acquired other addressees on its way to you: Max Thomas, who cared enough to collaborate; Lawrence Kramer, Robert K. Martin, Adalaide Morris, Fred Moten, Alan Nagel, Geeta Patel, Herman Rapaport, and Thomas Simmons, who cared enough to listen; Ned Brinkley, Thomas Christensen, William Cohen, Richard Dellamora, Emilio Englade, Maureen Felix, Sabine Golz, Keith Green, Richard Kaye, Robert Kopelson, Michael Lucey, Amy Nadel, and Michael West, who offered research assistance; Ellen F. Smith and Helen Tartar, who offered editorial assistance; Douglas Fishback and Maryann Rasmussen, who knew when to intervene; Cheryl Hetherington, who knew when not to; and Chris Freeman, who, for the sake of argument, is willing to remain under erasure.

I thank them all. I also wish to thank the University of Iowa, which gave me the wherewithal to begin this book; The Rockefeller Foundation, which enabled me to write part of it in Bellagio, Italy; and The Mellon Foundation, which enabled me to complete it at the University of Pennsylvania.

Contents

Preludes 1

1. Pianist Envy 7

   Intermezzo 35

2. Funérailles 37

   Intermezzo 59

3. Beethoven's Kiss 61

   Intermezzo 81

4. The Sexual Virtuoso 83

   Intermezzo 115

5. Music Lessons 117

   Intermezzo 137

6. Classified Information 139

   Coda 167

   Notes 171

   Works Cited 183

   Index 193

◦ M. de Charlus was only a Guermantes when all was said. But it had sufficed that nature should have upset the balance of his nervous system enough to make him prefer, to the woman that his brother the Duke would have chosen, one of Virgil's shepherds or Plato's disciples, and at once qualities unknown to the Duc de Guermantes and often combined with this lack of equilibrium had made M. de Charlus an exquisite pianist, an amateur painter who was not devoid of taste, and an eloquent talker. Who would ever have detected that the rapid, nervous, charming style with which M. de Charlus played the Schumannesque passage of Fauré's sonata had its equivalent—one dare not say its cause—in elements entirely physical, in the Baron's nervous weaknesses?

—Marcel Proust, *Cities of the Plain*

Beethoven's Kiss

PIANISM,
PERVERSION,
AND THE
MASTERY OF
DESIRE

~ My high school graduation took place in Carnegie Hall. I was the piano soloist and was to play Mendelssohn's Rondo Capriccioso. I'd spent months rehearsing the piece, usually at tempos too slow to do me any good. As it turned out, the performance seemed to go well— or at least as well as could be expected—and I received a standing ovation. But I'll never believe I deserved that ovation. I had told a number of friends to give me one and suspect that everyone else simply followed their lead. Just after the ceremony, when I met up with my family, my mother told me I'd made her very happy. Several hours after the ceremony, when I turned in for the night, I burst into hysterical, uncontrollable laughter—laughter my brother Steve took somewhat violent measures to suppress. And years after the ceremony, whenever I wanted to impress someone, I'd tell him I'd gotten a standing ovation in Carnegie Hall when I was sixteen but would neglect to mention that it had been at my graduation.

~ Throughout my childhood, and well into my adulthood, I used to imagine a movie camera filming my life. I was particularly inclined to activate this camera when I had to be good—when I had to do homework, to practice the piano, etc. (I was starring in a hagiography.) I also used to watch myself in a mirror when I felt wretched. I especially enjoyed seeing myself weep. (I was starring in a melodrama.) My family found these spectacles amusing.

~ My first sexual encounter occurred just before college graduation. David Abell, whom I had met in Battell Chapel (at a performance of *Saint Joan*) and who flirted with me during the next few days (we were both rehearsing Haydn's *Creation*—I was in the choir and David was in the pick-up orchestra), offered to walk me home after the concert. I was overcome with love and lust, but was terrified as well, because I didn't know what to do or say. When we got to my room, I managed to ask—somewhat sheepishly—whether he wanted to stay, "or what?" David responded, "Let's stop playing games." I didn't think I was playing anything. I didn't know how to flirt, didn't know how to seduce, and didn't know how to make love. He then came over to where I was standing and kissed me. When I opened my eyes, I saw myself in the mirror over my dresser. And even after we lay down, I imagined a movie camera in a corner of the ceiling and saw what that camera saw. I actually watched my own gay debut.

~ Dr. Train, the psychoanalyst my father had me see when Steve killed himself, once told me, after having determined that my mother hadn't caused my homosexuality, that the terrifying, dominating, and truly monstrous woman who had done so was Diana Graa, my first piano teacher. According to Train, Mrs. Graa convinced me I couldn't satisfy her fiendish, feminine desires—convinced me I was no good. Or at least not as

good as my older brother Bob. Bob the true child prodigy, Bob the one with perfect pitch, etc. Sad to say,
I believed him. Poor Mrs. Graa. She actually lost
her mind shortly after I entered Juilliard and stopped
studying with her. Not too long ago, Bob and I ran into
her in a Chinese restaurant. She was very charming
and polite, not at all terrifying, dominating, and monstrous, but every now and then she would turn to a
passer-by and mutter: "Those Kopelson brothers are
both *bitches*!"

~ When I asked Kathrine Parker, my teacher at Juilliard,
to teach me how to practice, she suggested I visualize
Vladimir Horowitz listening to me. Can you imagine
anything more incapacitating? How could Horowitz
ever like my playing? And can you imagine anything
more at odds with Miss Parker's other (constant) in-
junction: to stop looking at my fingers and start listening to myself? How could I listen to myself and try to
impress Horowitz at the same time?

~ I studied improvisation at Juilliard with Sylvia Rabinof, a friend of Mrs. Graa. Mrs. Rabinof taught us harmonic progressions over which we could make up various dances—mazurkas, polonaises, what have you. I
was never very good at this (I could only recreate the
progressions in either C major or A minor) and so was
relieved when Mrs. Rabinof, whose husband had just
died, was replaced by Miss Rosette. Miss Rosette
couldn't have cared less about tonal harmony and encouraged cacophonic abandon. I remember with particular fondness my *Playground Suite*, with its zany
"Slide-Upon" movement.

～ I don't fully understand my relationship to sentimentality. I used to have a rather immediate one: listening to Rachmaninov and weeping, etc. Now I'm somewhat ashamed of all that, somewhat proud of being ashamed, and somewhat ashamed of being ashamed. But I'm not, it seems, ashamed of *performing* the sentimental (as opposed to *being* sentimental). Or do I cite the sentimental simply in order to be sentimental? You'll never see me weep as I listen to Rachmaninov's third Piano Concerto. Or, God help me, to Saint-Saëns's "Organ" Symphony. (The me nobody knows.) You'll only ever see a facsimile of my real sentimental self. But when you do, know that it's a real facsimile.

～ When my parents disposed of the instruments in the family, Bob got the harpsichord as well as the Mason & Hamlin grand I'd used for 27 years, and I got Bob's Forster parlor grand. I mourn my loss and am experiencing sentiments you might appreciate. Steve, the brother I "crystallized," never returned the favor. I adored him, and he tormented me. I couldn't please him, couldn't make him desire my desire. The same is true of the Mason & Hamlin. I've always wanted to be, and have never been, as good a pianist as it is a piano. I've always wanted to deserve it—and now I know, for so I've been told, I don't. I'm still in love with that piano, and it will never love me back. I know what I have to do, though. Unless I can come to love—to crystallize—my new, inferior instrument (and I fear it's been tainted by Bob's superior touch), I must save my pennies and buy a Bösendorfer. Of course, it won't love me either, at first. But, who knows, perhaps someday . . .

∼ I've just remembered a dream I had when I was nine or so. I'm in a baroque theater, attending the premiere of an opera I've composed. The sets and costumes are gorgeous. The music is indescribable. I wake up and try to remember, to recompose, this music, music more beautiful than anything Mozart ever wrote, but I can't, of course. Did I dream an opera—at an age when I dreamt of being a virtuoso, and long before I ever dreamt of being a diva—because I knew even then that in order to express myself I had to make music sing, make the *piano* sing? And is that dream—my real, my imaginary, my lost plenitude—the impossible standard against which I've measured my subsequent "accomplishments"?

CHAPTER 1

ꙩ *Pianist Envy*

No, I never knew him. I saw him once, from
a distance, at the restaurant Lutétia: he was
eating a pear and reading a book. So I never
knew him; but there were a thousand things
about him that interested me.

Roland Barthes, *The Grain of the Voice*

ꙍ Roland Barthes, a writer I can't but love, never met André Gide, a writer I can. But imagine what might have happened if he had. September 1932. Gide, out for a late afternoon
stroll, notices a young *lycéen* reading *Le Temps retrouvé* and,
emboldened by the concurrence of fine weather and good
health, decides to cruise the boy. He takes an adjacent seat,
sighs, pretends to notice the book's title, and mentions that
he'd known the author personally. Barthes, who recognizes
Gide but thinks better of saying so, asks whether, in light of
that intimacy, he has reason to believe "Marcel" has been less
than honest about his sexuality. Gide, impressed by the boldness and cunning of the question, as well as by the charm of
the feigned ignorance (for it's clear the boy *must* know who
he is), suggests they continue this discussion at his home, over

tea and cookies. Barthes accepts the invitation, of course—in large part because, oddly enough, he finds the old man somewhat attractive.

Gide's rooms are cozy and his refreshments are tasty, but despite the structural implications of the rendezvous, neither party manages a sexual overture. Intercourse, to their mutual frustration, remains literary. Consequently, when Barthes asks his host to play something on the piano, Gide, thinking that music making, which will allow him to reveal hidden talent, passion, and sensitivity, might do the trick, obliges. He makes an unwise selection, however—the Chopin Barcarolle. His performance, as is so often the case when he plays for someone, is completely inept. Barthes, unintentionally cruel, asks whether the piece is harder than it sounds. Gide, intentionally cruel, suggests Barthes play something as well. Hoping to rekindle the erotic interest Gide's poor performance has extinguished, Barthes attempts the last movement of the Schumann Fantasie but, even though the piece isn't very difficult, fails to do it justice—a failure of which he, like Gide, who considers both the rendition and the taste evidenced by the selection to be far worse than his own, is well aware. The rendezvous is now irreparable. Barthes says he must be going, and Gide has no choice but to let him go. Before he does so, however, Gide calls Schumann "unbearable," offers Barthes a copy of his essay on Chopin, and suggests they get together again soon. After Barthes leaves, Gide eats dinner, practices the Barcarolle for two hours, and writes in his journal that he's "perfected" it. Barthes walks home, eats dinner, climbs into bed, reads a few more pages of Proust, masturbates, and waits for his mother to come kiss him goodnight.

It's not a pretty picture—but neither is the picture of these two getting it together. By some standards (mine), Gide and

Barthes were sexual amateurs. Gide loathed both anal and oral sex, never mastered *frottage*, and stuck to mutual masturbation, a technique he learned early in life. "[I] only understand pleasure face to face, reciprocal and without violence, and [am satisfied] by the most furtive of contacts," he writes in *Si le grain ne meurt* (346), an autobiographical account of more than one youthful transgression. And while Barthes offers no such description of his sexual repertoire, we do know, from *Incidents*, that he wasn't particularly good at arranging rendezvous and that, when he did arrange them, piano or no piano, he wasn't particularly likely to have the sex, let alone inspire the love, he so craved. In and of itself, however, this sexual amateurism, to use the term figuratively, isn't especially interesting. Plenty of gay men, including ones now called with more than a little irony professional homosexuals, probably feel their sexual performances leave something to be desired. What is interesting are the ways in which the literal status— or, as will be seen, non-status—of these gay writers as amateur pianists speaks to their figurative status as amateur homosexuals. What is interesting is the similarity, if not the identity, of their vexed relations—social, sensual, conceptual—to their non-virtuosic piano playing and their vexed relations to their non-virtuosic sexualities. A similarity or identity that will, I suspect, come as no surprise to the practicing music lover.

But before I describe what I claim to find interesting—an assertion that, insofar as it invites critical scrutiny, is itself performative and that involves its own (or, rather, my own) performance anxieties (for you may not find this very interesting after all)—allow me two self-defensive digressions. First, I'm not using Gide and Barthes to underscore the homophobic equation of homosexuality and failure (e.g., the straight-laced view of homosexuality as an inadequate imitation of heterosexuality or the pseudopsychoanalytic view of it as arrested development). I am, however, suggesting that while it's important to *celebrate* sexuality and gender as performative, it's also important to realize, or to be reminded, both that we don't always perform our selves very well and that our sexual failures, for want of a better word, can be quite as remarkable as our sexual successes. Second, I must acknowledge, for my unsubtle digs have probably made it clear, that I have a strange, but far from unique, investment in representing, if not believing, myself to be a better (i.e., queerer) gay man, as well as a better pianist, than either Gide or Barthes. There are probably many reasons why I have this investment, most of which escape me and one of which is far too personal to divulge. Let's just call it a male thing and leave it at that. But I've no doubt that on some, and perhaps the most important, level it's all too analogous to the equally strange, and equally commonplace, investment these writers have in being seen as better gays and better pianists than it's fair to assume they really were.

So, to begin, a fairly obvious but profoundly significant piece of conventional wisdom—in other words, an ideological given. Romantic pianists express themselves. This was true of the masters—Chopin, Liszt, Schumann, Rachmaninov—for whom such self-expression was more or less unproblematic. And it's true of their devotees—virtuosos like Horowitz and Rubinstein, amateurs like Gide and Barthes—for whom such self-expression is complicated by the fact that interpreters are also supposed to communicate *composers'* intentions. You may laugh when I sit down at the piano, but when I start to play (the "Moonlight" Sonata, according to the ad), you will see and hear, to quote Theodor Adorno, "a soul that bears witness to itself" (*Mahler* 130). I, however, will hear and feel that soul. By playing Beethoven, Romantic Beethoven, I *sense* my-self—my authentic, essential self. And if you happen to be there, I help you sense myself as well. (We may of course try to *make* sense of that self, to comprehend it, to read it pro-grammatically, but need not, and perhaps should not, do so in order to appreciate its expression.) Or, rather, we both sense my authentic, essential, *sexual* self, sexual identity being the touchstone of post-Romantic subjectivity. (We all believe, in-cluding those of us who are pianists, that our truest selves have specific sexualities—hetero, homo, take your pick.) Of course, it's too late to sense the sexual selves Gide and Barthes ex-pressed, or tried to express, as amateur pianists. Gide never recorded himself, and Barthes seems to have erased the tapes he did make. But we can comprehend them. We can read them both programmatically and symptomatically.

Amateur gay male pianists have it rough. For one thing, they would play their way into a class that disparages them and into a gender they themselves disparage. Unlike virtuos-ity, a phallic power exercised by antibourgeois (or, to use a term critics favor, "aristocratic") artists, amateur pianism is an "accomplishment," a skill traditionally required of middle-class wives and daughters—a skill no self-respecting male, not even a gay male, who is presumed to be ladylike, should care to cultivate.[1] (Nineteenth-century French police used to call men arrested in public rest rooms both *amateurs* and *hon-teuses* [bashful girls].)[2] On the other hand, many self-respecting gays do wish to acquire the cultural capital, or "taste" (the task of differentiating taste and accomplishment I leave to others), associated with both vocal and instrumental music—capital they think they need to join bourgeois social clubs that never really admit them. Why else would a file clerk pay eighty dol-lars to hear Joan Sutherland? Why else, for that matter, would an underpaid academic buy a Bösendorfer? But unlike opera queens, who can't work their way into masculinity and out of the middle class by supplementing their expertise, queer pianists (some of whom, to confuse matters, are opera queens) can conceivably do both. For if they play like virtuosos, they transcend both the debased femininity of amateur accomplishment and, to their chagrin, the social class into which they've tried to climb, the social class to which they'd like to belong.

So it is with a combination of class pride and sexual shame —in other words, it is with a sense of "accomplishment"— that Barthes describes himself as having "all the false occupations of a middle-class maiden [*jeune fille bourgeoise*] in the nineteenth century" (*Roland Barthes* 52). Unless, of course, Barthes's middle-class delight ("I play like a *bourgeois!*") occludes, or perhaps compensates for, his second-sex despair ("I play like a *girl!*"). But there are other, more obvious reasons why gay pianists, especially ones who'd sooner be aristocratic than bourgeois (an unpopular group to which I myself belong), remain amateurs. Face it, girls, most of us don't play like Vladimir Horowitz (a terrific pianist but a terrible homosexual), because Horowitz is *special* and because it's *hard* to play like Horowitz. His level of virtuosity requires rare talent, serious instruction, and, beginning in early childhood (a time when, if one is gay, one may not know it), hours upon hours of daily practice. In other words, gay pianists who can't outplay femininity have their own incompetence to blame ("If only I were gifted; if only I had practiced")—even if, like Gide, they tend not to ("If only my *genes* were gifted; if only my *mother* had made me practice").

Gay pianists who, as mere amateurs, fail to master masculinity also fail to matter. Who needs bourgeois girls filling our homes with music when we have radios and stereos? Who wants to hear little Suzette butcher Gottschalk's *The Dying Poet* when we can hear Maurizio Pollini conquer Liszt's *Funé-railles*? Today's amateurs are useless misfits—outmoded characters who'd better be virtuosos if they want to be taken seriously, to be validated. No wonder they spend so much time practicing scales and arpeggios. Even if they can't imagine how nice it would be to transcend a class that demonizes them as homosexual, they do realize how nice it would be to win a game in which amateurs count as odd men out. And they may even realize that virtuosos, who are seen as both masculine and reproductive (think of a raucous boom box), are prized as more or less heterosexual, whereas amateurs, who are seen as both effeminate and nonreproductive (think of a broken music box—preferably one with a ballerina on it), are written off as more or less homosexual.

For today's amateurs *are* nonreproductive. They may play other people's music, but, to repeat myself, no one listens to them. (Amateurs tend to repeat themselves—too insecure to learn new repertoire, we play the same three pieces over and over.) Like masturbating children—characters nineteenth-century doctors saw as homosexuals' kissing cousins—amateurs play by, for, and with themselves. Virtuosos are public and gregarious, amateurs private and solitary. Virtuosos come to life in concert halls, amateurs in closets. Gide hated to perform, because he played badly—like "an ungifted child of twelve"—when he did (*Journals* 2: 196). But he loved to practice. He loved to "satisfy himself" at the keyboard (*Journals* 3: 79). So did Barthes, who associates such *jouissance* with a number of related autoerotic activities (rewriting text, disseminating paradox). It's tempting, of course, to construe masturbatory pianism as essentially gay or gay pianism as essentially masturbatory. I could, for example, compare the number of queer virtuosos who fled the stage (Vladimir Horowitz, Van Cliburn, Glenn Gould) with the number of straight ones who never retired (Arthur Rubinstein, Rudolf Serkin, Claudio Arrau). But the comparison, even if not invidious (unlike some, I'd make it in order to *transvalue* both masturbation and homosexuality), would be mistaken. Plenty of queer pianists bask in limelight (remember Liberace?), and plenty of straight ones don't (remember Leopold Godowsky?). My point is that *all* amateur pianists (male, female, gay, straight) are, insofar as we confuse autoeroticism and homoeroticism, masturbatory perverts. It's that gay pianism isn't *essentially* masturbatory. Like all amateurs, gay pianists who happen not to be virtuosos are *constrained* to be masturbatory. They're *confined* to musical closets, closets most of them (even though solitary self-expression has its rewards) would rather leave. Most gay pianists, that is, yearn, if not for the days when amateurs functioned as sound systems, then to play—and to play well—in public. "Oh," Gide writes, refusing to blame himself, "if only I had been better advised, guided, encouraged, forced, in my youth! If only the pleasure I get from this practice could be less selfish!" (*Journals* 3: 79).

Hence their pianist envy. Hence their phobic attraction to virtuosos who put them in their effeminate, useless place. Some gay writers are quite candid—and even quite campy—about this disability. Oscar Wilde begins *The Importance of Being Earnest* by having Algernon proclaim: "I don't play accurately—any one can play accurately—but I play with wonderful expression. As far as the piano is concerned, sentiment is my forte. I keep science for Life" (488). Marcel Proust, who sees both pianism and perversion as "nervous weakness," has Charlus tell Morel: "I never heard Chopin play. . . . I took lessons from Stamati, [who] forbade me to . . . hear the Master of the Nocturnes. . . . It was a proof of his intelligence. He had realized that I was a 'natural' and that I would succumb to Chopin's influence" (1: 986, 1042). Christopher Isherwood, in a similar vein, writes of a fictional alter ego: "[Peter's] teacher told him that he would never be more than a good second-rate amateur, but he only worked all the harder. He worked merely to avoid thinking, and had another nervous breakdown" (81). But unlike Wilde, Proust, and Isherwood, whose candor I attribute to their not having been pianists, Gide and Barthes never bring their celebrated sincerity to bear upon virtuosity. They never say "I wish I were a virtuoso." (I'll say it for them.) Instead, they overrate their playing. Gide does so by presenting himself as a closet virtuoso, by claiming, for example, to have "perfected" Chopin's G minor Ballade and Albéniz's *Iberia* (*Journals* 2: 45, 204)—outrageous claims admirers who never heard him play tended to believe. I can't imagine Gide himself believed these claims. Even though he avoided piano recitals and so couldn't compare his Albéniz with, say, Rubinstein's, he did recognize true virtuosity: "Mlle X. dash[ed] off with extraordinary assurance and charm, to perfection, a number of compositions by Chabrier and Debussy. . . . Small wonder after that that I don't like pianists! . . . [W]hen I hear them I become ashamed of my playing" (*Journals* 2: 265–66). And while Barthes doesn't exactly claim to be a closet virtuoso ("I have no technique, no speed. . . . I can sight-read music, but I don't really know how to play" ["Grain of the Voice" 217]), he does overrate amateurism itself.

Then again, so does Gide. Both writers overrate second-rate and underrate first-rate pianism—stunning deconstructive transvaluations with which (for political reasons) I sympathize, to which (for aesthetic reasons) I take exception, and

15

through which (for personal reasons) I'll continue channeling their sexual selves. But despite the fact that Gide and Barthes have a lot in common (weak lungs, dead fathers, Protestant mothers) and despite the fact that their transvaluations of amateurism, like their related transvaluations of perversion, serve similar self-protective, self-assertive purposes, both the transvaluations and the sexualities the transvaluations express are very different. As different as—well, not night and day. As different as Chopin and Schumann. As different as modernism and postmodernism. In other words, to anticipate my punchline and articulate my methodology, not so very different after all.

One difference is that whereas Barthes focuses on things amateurs do right, Gide focuses on things virtuosos do wrong. Where Barthes, for example, applauds amateur physicality (which makes him seem self-satisfied), Gide derides virtuoso velocity (which makes him seem self-dissatisfied). But this difference shouldn't obscure the fact that both men resent virtuosity—a resentment of which Gide, at least, is somewhat aware: "I hate virtuosity, but . . . in order to scorn it I should first like to be capable of it; I should like to be sure of not being the fox of the fable" (*Journals* 2: 266). Nor should it obscure the fact that both want virtuosos to play like amateurs, a desire I can only describe as perverse. Barthes, I admit, is rather vague about what amateur-like virtuosity would entail. All he knows is that virtuosos have become too perfect. Virtuosity "has suffered a mutilation . . . has become a somewhat chilly prowess, a perfect achievement (without flaw, without accident) in which there is nothing to find fault with, but which does not exalt" ("Loving Schumann" 294) and which "no longer offer[s] that style of the perfect amateur whose value we could still recognize in a [Dinu] Lipatti . . . because it stirred in us . . . the desire to make such music" ("Musica Practica" 262). Gide, however, is quite specific and by being specific makes amateur-like virtuosity sound truly abysmal. Gide feels virtuosos have mutilated Chopin by playing too quickly, too brightly, too freely, and too vocally. He would have them play "*much more slowly than is customary*" (*Notes* 37), "in an undertone, almost in a murmur" (*Notes* 23), without "that *tempo rubato* I dislike so much" (*Journals* 2: 108), and without "*phrasing* . . . and punctuating . . . the melody" (*Notes* 41)—remarks that make me glad he didn't record himself. Because if Gide practiced what he preached (and chances are he preached what he practiced), he probably *never* played any better than an ungifted child of—well, let's give him some credit—thirteen. Like Barthes, he probably played so badly as to make keen (or should that be pretentious?) listeners wish they *hadn't* sensed his sexual self. But I'm also glad the two of them did record these and other related remarks, because it's the remarks that make sense of, that help me comprehend, the sexual selves they probably didn't express very well at the keyboard.

Did they, in fact, *try* to express sexual selves at the keyboard? Do they, for that matter, think they have sexual selves, sexual souls, to express? Gide does. He feels he "betrays his truth [*livre ma vérité*]," his spirituality (*paysage intérieur*), by playing well (*Oeuvres complètes* 12: 565). Barthes, however, feels he betrays his body, his physicality. Romantic music involves "subtle movements of the body" and hence can't "be predicated *romantically*." Soul is simply a "romantic name for the body"—a "moral," as opposed to "corporeal," term that invites ideological misreadings of composers like Schumann ("Rasch" 303–8), a term for which amateurs, who aren't "preoccup[ied] with the *imago*, [with] the image one . . . project[s] of oneself," have no use ("Grain of the Voice" 217). Is Gide, then, essentially Romantic, and Barthes anti-essentially anti-Romantic? Not exactly. For one thing, the body Barthes senses is quite soulful. It knows postmodern pleasure, of course, but it also knows desire and rage—key features of any Romantic sensibility, gay or otherwise. The Barthesian body, by traversing tonality, "lives in breathlessness, haste, desire, anguish, the approach of orgasm, etc." ("Rasch" 309). It also lives in fury. The virtuoso's body, "trained, streamlined by years of Conservatory or career," and hence "incapable of 'beating' (as is the case with Rubinstein)," is "almost always . . . mediocre." "It is not a question of strength," Barthes explains, "but of rage: the body must pound . . . (this has been glimpsed here and there by . . . Horowitz)" ("Rasch" 303). (I don't know which is worse: Gide's masturbatory murmuring, or Barthes's Byronic banging.) For another, the body Barthes senses isn't necessarily his own, a fact reflected in predications that are thoroughly Romantic. This, for example, is Barthes on *Kreisleriana*: "I hear Schumann's body . . . in the first variation, it curls up into a ball . . . in the second, it stretches out" ("Rasch" 299). This is Hans von Bülow on Chopin's E minor Prélude: "[I hear] one of the paroxysms to which [the composer] was subject . . . in the left hand . . . his heavy breathing, . . . in the right hand the tones of suffering wrung from his breast" (Schonberg, *Great Pianists* 137). These strikingly similar accounts are equally programmatic, equally representative of the nineteenth-century notion that instrumental music denotes incidents, images, thoughts, and feelings—a notion Gide, surprisingly enough, finds perplexing.

Even though Gide sees piano playing as self-expressive and Chopin, his favorite composer, as proto-impressionistic ("Before Debussy . . . I do not think that music was ever so shot through with the play of light, with the murmur of water, with

wind and foliage" [*Notes* 30]), he takes the anti-Romantic, an-
tiprogrammatic position that music "loses its real meaning
when it tries to take on too definite a meaning" (*Journals* 2:
100). Too definite? What could be more definite than "the play
of light" or "the murmur of water"? Feelings, of course. (What
else would you expect from someone with a dissociated sensibility?) Whereas most composers "start with an emotion
[and try] to express it," Chopin, "a perfect artist, starts with
notes" (*Notes* 30). But not just any feelings. Music is too meaningful, too significant when it specifies *sentimentality*, a feeling modernists like Gide find both inauthentic and "horrifying" (*Journals* 2: 204). Which explains why Gide rejects rubato. "Radio from the Tour Eiffel. An unknown pianist
(unknown to me) comes and murders Chopin's seventeenth
Prélude. Are there people who go into raptures over this? I see
nothing in it but an almost hideous vulgarity, affectation, and
stupid sentimentalism. Why hasten the tempo in the middle
of each measure? Can't it be seen that such false agitation drives
out all the charming mystery of the piece?" (*Journals* 3: 25) Or
does it explain the rejection? Perhaps the unknown virtuoso
has simply mastered the Romantic sentimentality Gide, on
some level, would like to carry off as well.[3] (The Gide nobody
knows. The Gide Gide himself may not know.) Perhaps he
manages to project the pathos Gide introjects—pathos that,
handled by an amateur, usually comes across as self-pity. Unless, of course, the amateur is someone like Barthes, someone
who in his *professional* capacity (in his *non*musical discourse)
transcends modernist antisentimentality. Someone who can
impersonate a lovelorn maiden without feeling sorry for himself—and without feeling ashamed.

Why then does Barthes write: "The Amateur . . . establishes
himself *graciously* (for nothing) in the signifier: in the imme-

diately definitive substance of music, of painting; his praxis usually involves no *rubato* (that theft of the object for the sake of the attribute); he is—he will be perhaps—the counter-bourgeois artist" (*Roland Barthes* 52)? Why, like Gide, does he link rubato to significance, to the "too definite," the too meaningful? Not because rubato signifies sentimentality, the reintroduction of which into "the politico-sexual field" Barthes calls "the *ultimate* transgression . . . the transgression of transgression itself" (*Roland Barthes* 65–66), but because it signifies significance. Rubato requires predication—adjectives, "attributes," inauthentic and horrifying stereotypes from which both musical and sexual subjectivity must be liberated. "Music . . . immediately receives an adjective . . . [a] predicate . . . by which the subject's image-repertoire protects itself against [loss]: the man who furnishes himself or is furnished with an adjective is . . . constituted; music has an image-repertoire whose function is to reassure, to constitute the subject, who hears it" ("Grain of the Voice" 267–68). Some subjective attributes, however, are sacrosanct. Even though Barthes claims to hate all stereotypes ("a pure language tactic, which is deployed *in the air* without any strategic horizon" [*Roland Barthes* 162]), he never deconstructs, and often reconstructs, stereotypes his amateur "body" finds too useful, and too pleasurable, to renounce—stereotypes with which his amateur soul (protecting its image-repertoire, but not projecting its *imago*) wishes to furnish itself and for which it listens, lovingly and programmatically, to Schumann. To sentimental, desirous, enraged Schumann. But rubato *does* signify sentimentality—a fact of which Barthes, like Gide, is well aware. It also signifies desire. (Think of Wagner's *Tristan und Isolde*, of Puccini's *La Bohème*.) So if Barthes does constitute himself as enraged by pounding away at Schumann but doesn't constitute himself as desirous and sentimental (attributes he happens to cherish) by using rubato, we can assume that he, like any amateur, knows how to pound, but not how to "hasten the tempo in the middle of each measure." Rubato, as any piano teacher will tell you, is a technique few amateurs master. Unlike pounding, a rather unmediated expression of "bodily" rage, rubato is an extremely mediated, an extremely artful expression of "bodily" desire and sentimentality—one even pianists who want to come across as desirous and sentimental (in Barthes's case, as *transgressively* desirous and sentimental) won't attempt for fear of coming across badly.

By the way, "hastening the tempo [*presser le mouvement régulièrement*] in the middle of each measure" is a rather misleading description of rubato. Rubato involves deceleration as well as acceleration and usually crosses bar lines. Gide's unconventional focus on haste (most people think rubato means "slow down," not "speed up") speaks, of course, to an envious realization that he can't play quickly, to the *self*-loathing with which he calls virtuoso velocity "intolerable haste [*précipitation*]" (*Notes* 56), but it also speaks to the fact that his sexuality is quite cautious. It speaks to the fact that—as both pederast and pianist—he wants to know where he's going and how he'll get there. Barthes's sexuality, however, is quite hasty, quite "breathless" ("Rasch" 309). Like Wayne Koestenbaum, Barthes demands of jouissance "little more than an impression of speed," little more than an "illusion that [he's] moving toward an end / Unseen by all but the wisest spectators" ("Answer" ll. 45–47). Which helps explain why he loves Schumann. (You'd think a pianist who, like Gide, can't play quickly, would want Schumann played slowly. Barthes has a different, and to my mind astonishing, way of coping with this incapacity: Schumann, he claims, "implies a technical *innocence* very few artists can attain" and "lets his music be fully heard only by someone who plays it . . . badly" ["Loving Schumann" 294–95]. Barthes listens to recordings of his own playing and, "after an initial moment of lucidity in which I perceive one by one the mistakes I have made," hears, "however pretentious it may seem to say so, the *Dasein* . . . of Schumann." He listens to Vladimir Horowitz or Sviatoslav Richter, and "a thousand adjectives come to mind." "I hear *them*," Barthes writes, "and not . . . Schumann" [*Roland Barthes* 55–60].) Where Gide finds Schumann's gaiety "hasty [*sommaire*]" and "feverish [*fébrile*]" (*Notes* 30; *Journals* 1: 32), Barthes finds it as blissfully insignificant as the absence of rubato. The German word *rasch*, he writes, "signifies only: *quick, fast (presto)*. But I . . . add to it the truth of the signifier: as if I had a limb swept away, *torn off* by the wind, whipped toward a site of dispersion which is precise but unknown" ("Rasch" 311). As if his sexual body were hastened toward fragmentation, dismemberment, and dissemination. Or maybe not. Just as Barthes clings to the notion that his soul makes a certain sense (clings to attributes like "enraged," "desirous," and "sentimental"), he also clings to the notion that his body makes a certain sense—a certain presymbolic, *maternal* sense. *Rasch*, which represents "the explosion of the *Muttersprache* in musical writing," also represents the "restoration of the body" ("Rasch" 310).

And what of Gide's body? What of Gide's desirous body? (I confess I'd rather consider Barthes's body than Gide's, even though they're similar—unwell, unathletic, unbeautiful. I simply prefer Barthes's self-affirming if quasi-fictive hedonism to Gide's self-denying if quasi-fictive asceticism.) What *non*spiritual truths does Gide use music to betray? For we know he feels music sexually, if not quite sentimentally. Chopin's music in particular, of course. (If only virtuosos like Alfred Cortot felt so too: Cortot, whose Préludes lack authentic—"rich, disturbing, indecent"—sensuality [*Journals* 3: 76, 80].)[4] Why "of course"? Gide, having discovered the two in one fell swoop (at age 24, in Algiers), associates Chopin with pederasty. He associates the transgressive pleasure of loving Chopin, whom his mother saw as "pernicious" (Métayer 72), with the transgressive pleasure of loving dark-skinned boys, whom she saw as perverted. (Unlike Mme Barthes, Mme Gide can't be said to have restored her son's body.) Which may explain why Gide places Chopin, who "proposes, supposes, insinuates, seduces, persuades . . . [and] almost never asserts" (*Notes* 24), in a position of erotic abjection—in the position, in other words, of a foreign concubine. For Gide does indeed colonize Chopin: "Though I may recognize in Chopin's work a Polish inspiration, a Polish spring, I am also pleased to recognize in this raw cloth a French cut, a French fashion" (*Notes* v).[5] Not that Gide ever recognizes any such "recognition" as masterful. He "perfects" Chopin but never dominates him. (It's virtuosos, he claims, who beat composers, and audiences, into submission—whose "sovereign" agility leaves us "dazzled and insensitive" [*Journals* 3: 412].) And like many sexual tourists, Gide has a pastoral, ahistorical conception of intercontinental intercourse. His lovemaking is "reciprocal and without violence." His love affairs, to cite Leo Bersani, are "belatedly contaminated by power from elsewhere" (221). (It's sodomites, he claims, who see sexual congress as a power play.) Barthes's egalitarianism is no less spurious. Sexual identities should be liberated from meaning, "including from transgression as meaning" (*Roland Barthes* 133), so that no one (heterosexual) identity is at a significant advantage. Unless, of course, that liberation impinges upon the stereotypical prerogatives of men who cruise for tricks. ("Tricking" and "cruising" are Barthes's gay male figures for sexual senselessness.) Amateurs, he writes, "engage in painting, music, sport, science, without the spirit of mastery or competition" (*Roland Barthes* 52). Unless, of course, we're talking about envious amateurs who devalue virtuosity.

Gide's asceticism, however, has nothing to do with the transgressive pleasure of mastering minions mommy doesn't like very much. It has to do with the conventional pleasure of self-control. Barthes, who's less puritanical, doesn't even bother to "finger" properly. "[I] reject the tedium of training," he writes, "[because] I want an immediate pleasure" (*Roland Barthes* 70). Gide, however, feels the body, the perverse body, should be disciplined as well as indulged. Pederastic affairs are limited to Algiers, a site of licit, contained transgression. Pianistic affairs are limited to Chopin, a composer Gide finds equally carnivalesque. But even Chopin, and even the rehearsal of Chopin, requires self-restraint. Chopin should be played like an eighteenth- and not a nineteenth-century composer. Whereas "virtuosos . . . bring out Chopin's romanticism," Gide admires the "masterful subservience [*asservissement magistral*]" with which Chopin "reduc[es] the undeniable romantic contribution" to classicism (*Journals* 3: 412–13). He should be played, in other words, as if he were Mozart, and not as if he were Schumann. Schumann can't quite get a hold of himself—his laughter is surrounded by "sobs." Chopin, however, "through and beyond . . . sadness . . . attains joy"—"calm," "crystalline" joy that "joins hands with that of Mozart" and "in which all the emotions [are] celestially transposed" (*Journals* 1: 32; *Notes* 30). Rehearsal is equally disciplinary. Learning Chopin—for that matter, learning Bach, Mozart, Schumann, etc.—represents a mastery of unruly impulses, or to quote one critic, "une méthode corrective aux mouvements impatients de la sensibilité et du désir" (Wald-Lasowski 167).

Gide, like Alissa in *La Porte étroite*, enjoys practicing the piano because he enjoys "overcoming . . . difficulty" (*Straight Is the Gate* 203–4).

Given this hatred of self-indulgence and given his hatred of rubato, Gide's position on improvisatory pianism is somewhat baffling. It's also somewhat Barthesian. Even though Gide disparages "false agitation," he encourages "trembling" (*Journals* 3: 293). Chopin should seem "improvised," he should be played with "uncertainty [and] without that unbearable assurance which . . . headlong movement carries with it" (*Notes* 21–22). Everything Chopin wrote, including the piano sonatas, should "keep the appearance of an impromptu [and convey] the impression of a successive discovery, of an advance into the unknown" (*Notes* 51). Except for the cautious denunciation of "headlong movement," Gide sounds almost "breathless." He sounds like he's approaching the "site of dispersion" Barthes, too, calls "unknown." Unfortunately, Gide never really throws caution to the winds. He never really "advances into the unknown," because when all is said and done, he gets his bearings—and settles down. Where Barthes sees improvisation as "closed to any general meaning, to any notion of fate, to any spiritual transcendence: in short a pure *wandering*, a becoming without finality" ("Romantic Song" 291), Gide sees it as *open* to general meaning, as a becoming *with* finality. He sees it as trips "adventurous souls" take along paths that, although not "blazed in advance," are recognizable in retrospect, amid landscapes that gradually "reveal themselves" (*Notes* 23), and toward destinations that, to invoke a fellow traveler, look more like Kansas than Oz.

Why, then, embrace improvisatory pianism at all? Why make Chopin seem spontaneous when you'd have him sound classical? For one thing, Gide likes to present himself as original. He'd have Barthes think him authentic by creating, and not recreating, the Barcarolle. Barthes presents himself as original as well, which is why I have him play the Fantasie ("the *Fantasy*, Schubertian or Schumannian: *Fantasieren*: at once to imagine and to improvise . . . to hallucinate" ["Romantic Song" 291]). But whereas Gide sees his originality as pre-textual (as belatedly contaminated by discourse), Barthes sees his as post-textual (as coterminous with a move beyond significance— beyond stereotypical subjectivity). Another reason why these writers embrace improvisation is that they see perversion as both furtive and extemporaneous. Queers are constrained to keep (it) to themselves and to make themselves up as they go along. (Needless to say, the fact that we have trouble following sexual scripts has something to do with the fact that they're not matters of public record.) The same is true of queer pianists who express themselves. (Ivo Pogorelich comes to mind.) Which explains Glenn Gould's identificatory misalliance of two singers I find rather insufferable. (One's too timid, the other too brazen.) "Like Schwarzkopf," he writes, "Streisand [leaves] no phrase . . . to its own devices, . . . one is simply unable to chart an *a priori* stylistic course on her behalf. Much of the *Affekt* of intimacy—indeed, the sensation of eavesdropping on a private moment not yet wholly committed to its eventual public profile—is a direct result of our inability to anticipate her intentions" (74).

Listening to a Gould recording is, in fact, like eavesdropping on a private moment. The playing is improvisatory, of course—but I'm not referring to the playing. I'm referring to the singing, which is so loud and so bad, it's hard to believe he knew he'd been taped. Unlike Gould, however, Gide doesn't see improvisatory pianism as especially vocal. Nor does he see it as especially orchestral. Whereas virtuosos approach the instrument transcendentally (Alfred Brendel, for example, claims it should evoke "an orchestra, or . . . a voice, [or] sounds of other worlds" [Mach 26]), Gide thinks pianos should sound like pianos. The term "well-tempered piano," he writes, "should be taken to mean that it does not try to give itself out as something other than what it is" (*Notes* 110). Given how hard it is to make pianos sing (pianos are percussive and don't produce sustained tones) and how hard it is to have them imitate orchestras (a feat dependent upon pedal control and manual dexterity few non-virtuosos attain), I could ascribe this anti-transcendentalism to Gide's amateurism alone. But I can think of other, and equally significant, ascriptions as well—ones unrelated to the authenticity with which Gide associates his anti-transcendentalism. (If Gide really wants to make an honest instrument of the piano, why does he prefer playing transcriptions to hearing the songs, operas, ensembles, and symphonies transcriptions only approximate?) For one thing, Gide dislikes both vocal and orchestral music. He loathes Bellini, whom Chopin emulated, and thinks the important thing about Beethoven is the "quantity" of sound (*Journals* 1: 345). For another, Gide's antitranscendentalism represents a displaced rejection of asceticism. Maybe he doesn't play Chopin like Liszt ("Have you ever heard actors declaiming Baudelaire as if they were doing Casimir Delavigne? [Well, virtuosos] play Chopin as if it were Liszt" [*Notes* 20]), and maybe he doesn't care to be "smothered" by Wildean voluptuaries (*Immoralist* 112), but he does embrace what Barthes would call the grainy body (the sexy, "homogenous" timber) of the piano in ways virtuosos simply do not (*Journals* 3: 25). What else could account for the odd juxtaposition of these two thoughts: "For Chopin only the quality [of sound matters] (pianissimo in the Barcarolle). No more limpid diamond. No pearl of finer water. (To say after the Algiers night in the *Mémoires* [*Si le grain ne meurt*].) How often the joy of love . . . left me in such an exasperated, atrocious delirium of all the senses that, for a long time afterward, I could not relax and overexerted my frenzy, not consenting to be released, to take leave of the instant, but insatiably avid and as if pursuing through pleasure something beyond pleasure" (*Journals* 1: 345).

If Gide embraces the body of the piano in ways virtuosos do not, he also embraces it in ways Barthes does not. Not that Barthes would have the piano sound orchestral. In fact, and for reasons Barthes relates to amateur privacy and virtuoso inadequacy, he claims it can't: "The amateur cannot master Beethoven's music, not . . . because of the technical difficulties [but because] the mimetic pulsion [is orchestral and] hence . . . escapes the fetishism of a single element (voice or rhythm): the body seeks to be total; thereby, the notion of an intimist or family *praxis* is destroyed: to *want* to play Beethoven is to project oneself as an orchestra conductor. . . . Beethoven's oeuvre abandons the amateur and seems, initially, to summon up the new romantic deity, the interpreter. Yet here there occurs a new disappointment: who (what soloist, what pianist?) plays Beethoven well?" ("Musica Practica" 264). He would, however, have it sound vocal. He'd have the piano sound like a human voice. Like the speaking, or nearly speaking, voice—of someone else, someone gay men (Proustians in particular) find it hard to forget.

Contrary to what you'd expect of an opera (or *Lieder*) queen, Barthes doesn't hear piano playing as singing.[6] He hears it as speaking, a formulation you can construe as either paradoxical or stereotypical. (Making the piano "sing" is a cliché of the twentieth century; making it "speak," a cliché of the nineteenth century.) "What does the body do," he asks, "when it enunciates (musically)?" "[It] speaks, it declaims, it doubles its voice: *it speaks but says nothing*: for as soon as it is musical, speech—or its instrumental substitute—is no longer linguistic but corporeal; what it says is always and only this: *my body puts itself in a state of speech: quasi parlando*" ("Rasch" 305–6). But the body—Barthes's hasty, impromptu, non-rubato body —doesn't really double *its* voice in an attempt to express itself by "saying nothing." Its own voice is too grotesque for any such double duty. Barthes has, he says, a "feeling of strangeness (sometimes of antipathy) [when] hearing his own voice: reaching us after traversing the masses and cavities of our own anatomy, it affords us a distorted image of ourselves, as if one were to glimpse our profile in a three-way mirror" ("Listening" 255). It doubles—although Barthes never (mis)recognizes it—the voice of the mother. *Muttersprache.* The Barthesian body signifies its senseless, sensuous, and dismembered self by using Schumann ("the man with two wives—two mothers?—the first of whom sang and the second, Clara [Wieck], visibly gave him abundant speech" ["Rasch" 310]) to impersonate (wherein lies a second, more fundamental displacement) the one woman who ever sees it whole, the one woman who ever lets it see itself whole. (This transcendental displacement is more conventional than Gide's antitranscendental one: Barthes impersonates a parent, whereas Gide impersonates a piano.)

But Barthes never quite impersonates the mother. He never really has her express himself at the keyboard. "*Quasi parlando* (I take the indication from one of Beethoven's *Bagatelles*): this is the movement of the body *which is about to speak* . . . the instrument (the piano) speaks without saying anything, in the fashion of a mute who reveals on his face the inarticulate power of speech. [The] voice speaks in order to say nothing but the

29

measure (the meter) which permits it to exist—to emerge—
as signifier" ("Rasch" 306–7).[7] To emerge as signifier, to verge
on utterance. Barthes can't quite betray himself, or rather can't
quite have his mother do so, because, like Wilde, he sees both
truth and the truth of (homo)sexual subjectivity as paradoxical—as too personal, too private to divulge. (Truths would
be *doxical* if anyone other than Barthes believed them: "A *Doxa*
(a popular opinion) is posited, intolerable; to free myself of
it, I postulate a paradox; then this paradox turns bad, becomes
a new concretion, itself becomes a new *Doxa*" [*Roland Barthes* 71].) Which helps explain why, unlike Gide, he doesn't
seem to find his forced occupation of a musical closet *too* constrictive.

But it doesn't explain why, contrary to popular belief (contrary, in fact, to his own pronouncements), Barthes rejects
Wilde's view of subjectivity as thoroughly superficial. Or, to
put it another way, why he'd never celebrate sexuality as performative and then leave it at that. Even though Barthes sees
himself as both textual and post-textual—as both describable
and, with any luck, indescribable—he also sees himself as incredibly deep. (It's Barthes who's incredulous—whose sense
of himself as two-dimensional interrogates his sense of himself as profound.) When he claims Schumann comes across
played poorly, he means both composer and performer (Barthes, presumably) are men of substance, men who aren't always already discursive constructions. You're probably thinking: sounds a lot like Gide—Gide who sees himself as pre-textual, as belatedly contaminated by discourse. Think again.

Where Barthes understands bad Schumann, Gide can't stand
bad Chopin. "Play Beethoven, even Schumann, on an old tinny
piano, something will always remain. Play Chopin only on an
excellent piano. For the very reason that he never brings any-

thing superfluous, he needs everything in order to be adequate. He becomes himself only when perfect" (*Notes* 111). He needs more than an excellent piano, however. He needs an excellent pianist. "Bach, Scarlatti, Beethoven, Schumann, Liszt, or Fauré can be more or less well interpreted. One does not falsify their meaning [*signification*] by slightly distorting their character [*allure*]. Chopin is the only one who is betrayed [*qu'on trahisse*], who can be deeply, intimately, totally violated" (*Notes* 20). The only one other than Gide, that is. With Chopin, as with Gide, distinctions between meaning and character—between surface and depth, form and substance, signifier and signified—become, if not inapposite, problematic. Gide, in other words, is far more superficial, far more stylish than his essentialist advocates and anti-essentialist detractors would like to believe. Not, however, because he's been "smothered" by Wilde, but because "perfect" artists (Chopin, of course, and probably Cortot as well) and imperfect parents (I'm guessing, but it's a good guess) have made him feel, on a level I'd call profound, like a failure. In other words, Gide "betrays" himself at the keyboard in two senses of the word. He both expresses (*livrer*) and can't express (*trahir*) himself. He betrays his truth, but it's a sad one. Gide, like Chopin, "becomes himself only when perfect." But, unlike Chopin, he's never perfect, never as good as he's supposed to be. And contrary to *his* pronouncements, he knows it.

Now look what I've done. I've actually made myself—no, I still can't say I *love* Gide. I do, however, feel sorry for him. How sorry? Well, sorry enough to grant his unspoken wish. (I've never been a fairy godmother before, so keep your fingers crossed.) Imagine Gide *does* play Chopin perfectly. Imagine his Barcarolle does do the trick. But instead of imagining that sex act (as you may recall, it's not a pretty picture), imag-

ine how Barthes might envision a man who's mastered a composer for whom he himself has no particular predilection. One
reason Barthes loves Schumann is that his music tends to be
fragmentary. Schumann's forms seem broken, incomplete,
and disconnected—much like Schumann himself. And much
like Barthes himself, or so he'd have us think. Schumann, he
says, expresses the "decentering of the subject (a very modern
temptation) . . . by the carousel of his brief forms" ("Loving
Schumann" 296). He avoids classical structures, the sonata
form in particular, because they convey a false sense of organic
integrity and reinforce a conventional notion of psychosex-
ual growth. "I hear it said: Schumann wrote so many short
pieces *because he didn't know how to develop.* A repressive criticism: what you *refuse* to do is what you *can't* do. The truth is
more likely this: the Schumannian body does not stay in place
(a major rhetorical transgression). . . . The intermezzo [func-
tions] not to distract but to displace: like a vigilant sauce chef,
it keeps the discourse from 'setting,' from thickening, from
spreading, from returning obediently into the culture of development; [in other words, it] begins to criticize (to put in
crisis) the discourse which, under cover of art, others have
tried to put over on it, without it" ("Rasch" 300). Gide, however, is one of the repressive critics Barthes criticizes. Schumann's "developments," Gide writes (the scare quotes are his),
"are unbearable to me, however exquisite the motif may be,
and there are few of his compositions of which I would not
be glad to drop half" (*Journals* 2: 389). Which is one reason
he loves Chopin, who seems impromptu but isn't—whose
structures are both well organized and well developed. (Schumann is, in fact, far more extemporaneous than Chopin—
whereas Chopin composed music, Schumann transcribed im-
provisations.) Barthes might just glean this from Gide's per-

fectly self-expressive performance. He might, that is, envision the *imago* Gide projects as perfectly centered.

But I doubt *I'd* consider Gide centered, even if he'd ask me to. (So much for fairy godmothering.) I simply don't hear Chopin the way Gide and Barthes do. They perceive structural coherence and subjective integration. I perceive incoherence and disintegration. I realize it's an ignorant, amateurish perception but can't seem to transcend it. And for what it's worth, neither can Adorno, who'd envision any Chopin player, including Gide, as both *un*centered and *self*-centered.[8] Nor do I hear Schumann the way they do. Gide and Barthes perceive structural incoherence and subjective disintegration. I perceive coherence and integration. So if *I'd* heard Barthes's (once again, perfectly self-expressive) Fantasie, I wouldn't write it— or him—off as decentered. It's not that I'm astute enough to recognize latent integrity.[9] Schumann's music makes sense to me—more sense than music I happen to prefer (Chopin's, for example)—because I heard an awful lot of it as a child. Which means, I suppose, that I've an amateurish and therefore faulty sense of Schumannian structure—that Schumann coheres for me not because he's coherent, but because he's familiar. But isn't all sense of structure amateurish? Barthes would say so. He'd say that nothing really coheres, but some things seem (unbearably) familiar. He'd say, in other words, that discursive structures and piano virtuosos have a lot in common. They're both too damn perfect.

Intermezzo

↬ I've only given two solo recitals. Both were on Stein-
ways, and both were memorials. The first was dedicated
to Linda Turchin, a surrogate—or supplemental—
mother. If memory serves, the program, which included
works by Schumann, went rather well. (I've never listened to the tape and don't know if I'd hear anyone's, or
any one composer's, *Dasein* if I did.) The second was
dedicated to Steve, who, as luck would have it, had been
gay. That program, which included works by Chopin,
didn't go well. I'd begun too slowly, ended too quickly,
and even managed to ruin the "Aeolian Harp" Etude, a
piece I'd never found particularly difficult. I was discon-
certed, of course, but not depressed. I simply wanted to
know, and to correct, what went wrong, and so I re-
played the étude (on the Mason & Hamlin) as soon as I
got home. It was then that, for reasons that may be con-
nected to my not having ruined it this time, as well as to
my not having had Steve there to hear me (Steve, who'd
never cared for my playing), I burst into tears. My father, who did attend the repeat performance, seemed to
comprehend it—something I myself have yet to do.

CHAPTER 2

∿ *Funérailles*

Minor chords [open] to the Other,
whose unattainability induces weeping.

Theodor Adorno, *Mahler*

∿ When Maurizio Pollini does conquer *Funérailles*, whom
do I really hear? Who is it I hear when Youri Egorov plays it?
(I own a pirated recording.) Who when I play it? (Yes, "who,"
not "what," is it I hear, even though both questions solicit programmatic responses.) I hear the dead. I hear the men Liszt
had in mind—Hungarians killed in the 1848 revolution. I hear
Liszt as well. Chopin too. I hear Egorov, who died of AIDS. I
hear myself, who may or may not do so. I hear my brother,
who died many years ago. I hear my father, who died last summer.

Why Chopin? For one thing, Liszt wrote *Funérailles* shortly
after Chopin died. For another, he lifted those left-hand octaves from Chopin's A-flat major Polonaise—a theft to which,
shortly before his own death, Liszt himself attested ("this is

taken from Chopin's well-known Polonaise; however, I have done it . . . slightly differently" [Hamburger 104]), but to which some of his admirers, for reasons worth considering, would rather not. Whereas Alan Walker, for example, describes *Funérailles* as a "threnody for Chopin" that both resurrects ("brings back to life") the polonaise and represents the onset of Liszt's "posthumous *identification*" with the man ("Liszt's Musical Background" 61, emphasis added), Eleanor Perényi can't believe her ears. What "strange compulsion," she wonders, subtends Walker's "astounding statement that from 1849 to 1855, Liszt succumbed to a Chopin mania, a spooky, 'posthumous *inspiration*'?" These, after all, "were the years when Liszt was devoting himself to the orchestra, not the piano." And, at any rate, the Chopinesque section of *Funérailles*, a "composition [that] as a whole does not resemble Chopin in the least," probably refers to Felix Lichnowsky, another Polish friend. If Walker won't believe Perényi, why doesn't he just ask Rosemary Brown, the batty "English housewife who claims to receive daily visits from Liszt, [to take] musical dictation from [him, and to learn] information not otherwise known" (65, emphasis added).

Walker, who came to reject, if not the idea of a posthumous identification, then the idea that *Funérailles* should be heard as a threnody for Chopin, appears to have been intimidated by this homophobic attack. The "thunderous left-hand octaves [do] show more than a passing acquaintance with [the] Polonaise in A-flat major," Walker writes in his new Liszt biography, "but in light of what we know of the origins of *Funérailles* today, the link with Chopin must be seen as little more than a romantic fabrication" (*Liszt* 2: 73). We, however, needn't be cowed. If we want to hear *Funérailles* as a threnody for Chopin, we should do so. Nor need we turn Liszt's posthumous "identification," or rather his *desirous* identification, into an "inspiration." (I'm referring to Perényi's mistaken transcription.) Liszt wouldn't have. He lived in an age when male "homosociality" was far more homoerotic than we now know, or allow, it to be. Why else would he publish a dream about realizing he had to "merge with," "transform," and be transformed by a "tall, serious, and pensive" man ("still young, although his face was pale, his look intense, and his cheeks haggard") whose "breath animated my life," who "held the secret of my destiny," and who asked, "If it is a malevolent force that harasses and torments me, why these divine dreams, these inexpressible, voluptuous floods of desire?" ("Letter to Lambert Massart," *Gazette musicale* [1838], in *Artist's Journey* 95–97).

Liszt's dream date isn't exactly Chopin, of course. Chopin wasn't "tall," not even by early nineteenth-century standards. Nor was he "haggard," or at least hadn't yet become so, when Liszt recounted the dream. But why not entertain the notion that Liszt dreamed of "merging" with Chopin? He does describe *our* Chopin—the pathetic Pole with the hacking cough —rather well. In fact, the only aspect of our stereotypical and somewhat spurious conception of Chopin Liszt doesn't touch upon is his utter lack of virility. We tend to see, to hear, and to a certain extent to marginalize Chopin—the man and the music—as effeminate. The Nocturnes foster this impression, even though many of them aren't especially ladylike, as does our knowledge of the affair with George Sand, that notorious cross-dresser.[1] And I suspect it is this, more than anything else, that prevents Perényi from seeing eye to eye with early Walker. Those thunderous octaves are far too manly to be by Chopin (didn't he only write delicate salon pieces?) and far more indicative of the heroic death of a Pole who died in battle (Lichnowsky) than of the pathetic death of one who died of consumption. If Liszt must be "inspired" by a dead man, for God's sake let it be a man's man. (Incidentally, the fact that Perényi has Liszt consort with Lichnowsky at all indicates she doesn't have a problem with musical necrophilia per se. Then again, who does?)

Chopin himself sensed this gender trouble. He resented his feminization almost as much as do a number of contemporary pianists. Rubinstein, for example, claims to have rescued Chopin from the salon, and Edward Said (who considers the status of the "fully committed *amateur*" to be less "disabling [than] one might think" [xxi]) sees him as an "astonishing revolutionary" (59). Chopin never forgave Schumann for naming a nocturne-like and improvisatory section of *Carnaval* after him—not because he saw it as parodic, a line taken by several critics,[2] but because he saw it, and in particular Schumann's Chopinesque fingering of the Chopinesque filigree, as emasculating. (One late-nineteenth-century editor calls the fingering a "humorous imitation of [Chopin's] novel method" [Schumann, *Carnaval* 19]). Or so I'd like to think. Schumann's "Chopin" is simply too beautiful for anyone, including Chopin, to see it as parodic. It's so beautiful, in fact, and so much more in keeping with our stereotypical conception of Chopin than *Funérailles* that I can't help but hear it as an especially loving tribute.

As a matter of fact, Schumann's love for Chopin, or rather his identificatory desire for Chopin, did go further than Liszt's. Or at least it did so according to our rather panicky notion of "going too far." Schumann, in a review published shortly before Liszt's dream, describes being "carried along body and soul by the dark flood" of a Chopin waltz and telling "Beda" (Clara Wieck), his dancing partner, of their acquaintanceship. "And you have actually heard him," she asks, "and have even heard him speak?"

And now I told her what an unforgettable sight it was to see him at the piano, like a dreaming soothsayer, and how, as he played, one be-

came identified in one's own mind with his dream, and how he had
an iniquitous habit, at the end of each piece, of running a finger from
one end of the keyboard to the other in a disruptive glissando, as if
to break the spell, and how he had to spare himself because of his
delicate health, and so forth. She pressed herself ever more closely to
me, seemingly prompted by a combination of anxiety and pleasure,
and begged me to go on. O, Chopin, you charming heart-breaker! I
have never envied you—but now? In fact, Jeanquirit [the putative
addressee], I was stupid, nothing but the brush that brought the
sainted hero within kissing distance—yes, stupid. ("The Editor's Ball,"
Neue Zeitschrift für Musik [1837], in *Schumann on Music* 129–30)

Schumann's oneiric "identification," unlike Liszt's, involves
kissing, or being kissed by, Chopin. Clara, of course, is supposed to be the lucky lady, and Robert the odd man out. But
when nineteenth-century men fantasize about other men making love to their girlfriends—in other words, when they "homosocialize"—*cherchez la femme* isn't necessarily the final
word on the subject.[3]

As both *Funérailles* and *Carnaval* indicate, men who share
Walker's "strange," necrophilic, and Chopinesque "compulsion"—in other words, men who tend to reiterate Liszt's desirous identification—may feel they have to make a choice.
They may feel compelled to choose between Chopin's manly
body (the thunderous left-hand octaves only virtuosos handle well) and his womanly body (the delicate filigree even amateurs learn to finger). The first choice is, of course, the safe,
homosocial one, and the second the unsafe, homoerotic one.
On the other hand, they may neither have to, nor be able to,
choose at all. Listen to, or play, the G minor Ballade. Which
(dead) Chopin do you really care to cathect: the hyperfeminine one who used to play the E-flat major interlude or the
hypermasculine one who played the coda? (Not that Chopin
ever played very loudly. Sigismond Thalberg, having attended

a Chopin recital and then shouted all the way home, told one witness: "I need some noise, because I've heard nothing but pianissimo all evening" [Schonberg, *Great Pianists* 152].) Both Chopin's music and the dead body we imagine making that music, like the music and music-making bodies of other Romantic pianists, including Liszt, are completely androgynous, which may make it very difficult for hypermasculine, as well as for hyperfeminine, fans to take him all at once. But it may, in fact, make it relatively easy for gay men (and lesbians) who see themselves as androgynous "inverts" to do so.

Desirous identification, identificatory desire—is that what's going on here? Yes, but let's not rehearse the psychoanalytic explanation of this phenomenon. Let's just say we all spend a lot of time trying—and failing—to distinguish identification from desire. Like Wayne Koestenbaum, we all ask ourselves questions like, "Am I in love with Julie Andrews, or do I think I *am* Julie Andrews?" (*Queen's Throat* 18). We even ask them long after we think we've been oedipalized. Let's also say, along with Eve Kosofsky Sedgwick, that the main reason purportedly heterosexual men try to distinguish between the two is that they'd rather not desire men with whom they identify. And even though the current culture industry, no less homophobic than Western culture in general, does enable these men to feel they've managed to avoid having homosocial identifications problematized by homoerotic desires (Arnold Schwarzenegger, for example, packages himself in particularly unappealing ways), sentimental texts that feature pathetic young men, texts that tend not to be produced by the industry, almost never do. Sentimental readings, as Sedgwick argues, should be seen as relational, because they rely upon vicarious investments, or cathexes, most men find both exciting and unsettling:

The tacitness and consequent nonaccountability of the identification between sufferer and spectator [is] the fulcrum point between the most honorific and the most damning senses of "sentimental." For a spectator to misrepresent the quality or locus of her or his implicit participation in a scene—to misrepresent, for example, desire as pity, *Schadenfreude* as sympathy, envy as disapproval—would be to enact defining instances of the worst meaning of the epithet; the defining instance, increasingly, of the epithet itself.

In fact, every subcategory of the sentimental—including my personal favorite, "the morbid"—involves "spectatorial" and desirous identification (*Epistemology* 151).

Spectatorial, to be sure—but *auditory* as well. Haven't you ever had your heart broken by a disembodied voice? By Radames recognizing Aida and crying, "Tu . . . in questa tomba!" Or by Koestenbaum, who ends a poem devoted to a friend who died of AIDS with the lines:

> I meet Metro in his still-tended garden
> And I am wearing his clothes, given to me because
>   We are one size. I want to read Metro's lips
> For he is facing the invisible, and speaking
>   Eloquently of efforts taken too late.
> The many souls wandering in the air, not pinioned
>   As children are. I am too corporeal
> To hold the attention of one so weightless, to say,
>   In a tone of sad confusion, that the good
> Suit he wore in life fits me well, too well, like a
>   charm.
>   ("Answer" ll. 152–61)

Disembodied voices, even ones we hear while reading, are much easier to cathect than are voiceless bodies that, if not too unattractive, rarely resemble us. I'm in love with Koestenbaum, and to a certain extent think I *am* Koestenbaum, not because he's sexy (he's not my type) or because we look alike, but because I can see myself (re)writing *The Queen's Throat*. (As a matter of fact, I'm doing so right now.) Sedgwick, of course, does know that morbid fascination is auditory as well as spectatorial. After all, it is Sedgwick who traces her recent realization that the "impossible" and "gender-equivocal" first person of someone dead (Metro) or dying (Radames) can be "peculiarly potent" to having been "blown away" by a song about yet another dead man (Christ) in yet another garden— a realization I, who am in love with Sedgwick as well and who've been "blown away" by texts like *Funérailles*, feel compelled to reiterate (*Epistemology* 143).

Texts like *Funérailles*, however, aren't always disembodied. Whereas listeners may feel far more "corporeal" than (dead) composers, and may even feel more corporeal than (non-live) performers, pianists who play Liszt, Chopin, and Schumann do not. We sense, along with our own movements, the androgynous or "gender-equivocal" movements once made— and now being made—by Liszt, Chopin, and Schumann. Am I playing those octaves? Or is Liszt? Or is Chopin? Am I playing that filigree? Or is Schumann? Or is Chopin? It's hard to say. Pianists occupy other men's, and to some extent other women's, bodies—something that can't be said of listeners.[4] Nor can it be said of readers. (It can, however, be said of dancers.) For gay pianists—practicing homosexuals who don't panic when they find themselves desiring other men—this corporeal occupation can be rather erotic. (Am I in love with Chopin, or do I think I *am* Chopin? Or do I think I'm *shtupping* Chopin?) It can be erotic for nongay ones as well, of course, but they have another word for it: "aesthetic."

Pianists who reproduce dead men's gestures "speak," to use the nineteenth-century cliché, and "sing," to use the twentieth, on their behalf as well. (So do actors and singers.) In other words, the incorporation I find erotic involves vocalization. Or should that be, the incorporation I find *romantic*? To quote Julia Kristeva:

When the object that I incorporate is the speech of the other—precisely a nonobject, a pattern, a model—I bind myself to him in a primary fusion, communion, unification. . . . In being able to receive the other's words, to assimilate, repeat, and reproduce them, I become like him: One. A subject of enunciation. Through psychic osmosis/identification. Through love. (*Tales of Love* 26)

Maybe I shouldn't conflate love and desire. Maybe I shouldn't gloss "identificatory *desire*" with the phrase, "Am I in *love* with [Andrews-Koestenbaum-Sedgwick-Chopin]?" Isn't love supposed to be ideal, and desire less than ideal? Not exactly. We're talking about Romantic (nineteenth-century) experience here —Romantic erotics, Romantic aesthetics, Romantic sentimentality, Romantic sensibility, Romantic fabrication—and, according to the Romantics, "true love is the conjunction of concupiscence with affection." It's both "sensual" and "tender" (Gay 45). In other words, two of the three questions raised by my vocal incorporation of my favorite composer—"Am I in love with Chopin" and "Am I *shtupping* Chopin"—are pretty much the same question. The terms "erotic" and "romantic," however, barely begin to describe the gay experience of posthumous vocal embodiment. When Chopin and I become one subject of enunciation as well as one subject of mobilization, the degree to which I sense, sensualize, and sentimentalize his "impossible" presence is almost incalculable. I find myself making love to a dead man, a sad affair, to be sure, but one I also feel to be "peculiarly potent."

Sedgwick, of course, uses the phrase "peculiarly potent" to predicate cathexes of *disembodied* voices, which makes my citation understated and confusing. Is corporeal (and vocal) morbidity sexier than incorporeal (and nonvocal) morbidity, or isn't it? It is, but only gay pianists know this. The point of the understatement and confusion is that listeners, and in particular gay listeners, who don't play the piano hear the dead—and by "hear the dead" I still mean "sense, sensualize, and sentimentalize the 'impossible' presence of the dead"—as well. Or, if not quite "as well," then well enough. Well enough, that is, to know what Sedgwick and I mean by "peculiarly potent."

Who are the dead? Who, that is, besides composers and the men they cathect? Or rather, to trope *apophrades* (Harold Bloom's metaleptic trope of tropes) by revisiting its uncanny vehicle, who besides composers and the big, "strong" men they'd have (yet not have) "return" from the grave?[5] For, if I do say so myself, transumptively as well as presumptively, I think I've exhausted—and exhumed—that topic. To begin by making a more or less nonrandom selection: the dead include one's parents. Like many gay men, I'm a "mama's boy"—or think I used to be one. (I equivocate, because I'm torn between Barthes's "semioclasmic" rejection of all such stereotypes and Koestenbaum's transvaluative acceptance.)[6] I happen not to hear my mother when I play or listen to piano music, because she's still alive. I do, however, hear Linda Turchin, the motherly neighbor who died when I was sixteen, and so can identify with Barthes, a mama's boy (although he never cared to admit it) who did outlive his mother and who did hear her *Dasein* when he played, or listened to, Schumann. (It's not clear which.) Consider *Camera Lucida*, a text Barthes "derives" from a snapshot (the "Winter Garden Photograph") that captures his mother's essence and reproduces her presence—or, to use his terminology, that "accomplishes the unheard-of identification of reality ('that-has-been') with truth ('there-she-is!')" (73, 113).

This Winter Garden Photograph was for me like that last music Schumann wrote before collapsing, that first *Gesang der Frühe* which accords both with my mother's being and my grief at her death; I could not express this accord except by an infinite series of adjectives, which I omit, convinced that this photograph collected all the possible predicates from which my mother's being was constituted. . . . The Winter Garden Photograph was indeed essential, it achieved for me, utopically, *the impossible science of the unique being.* (*Camera Lucida* 70–71)

I find this passage remarkable for a number of reasons. First, *Gesänge der Frühe* (Op. 133; Songs of early morning) weren't the last compositions Schumann wrote before "collapsing." I do, however, understand the sentimentality that turns treasured texts into dying declarations. ("Liszt lifted those left-hand octaves from Chopin's Polonaise—a theft to which, *shortly before his own death,* Liszt himself attested." Linda, shortly before *her* death, heard me play Schumann's *Papillons* and paid one final compliment: "What a beautiful waltz!") Second, Barthes can't quite register the fact that the first *Gesang der Frühe* sounds like Brahms. It even features a retrograde version of a theme found in an early Brahms sonata (Op. 2). Did Barthes find his mother inexplicably Brahmsian? If so, what would that predication mean? Does he omit it, along with every other adjective, because he doesn't care for, or cathect, the "Brahmsianicity" of *Brahms*? And why shouldn't he cathect Brahms, when Schumann, whom Barthes does "love," did? Third, "truth," for Barthes, is fundamentally inexpressible. It's too private and too paradoxical to divulge. Yet, "there-she-is!" There she is, in the Winter Garden Photograph Barthes fails to reproduce (a typical refusal: Barthes won't speak his mind for fear we'd come to see what he means).[7] There she is, in the *Gesang der Frühe* anyone can choose to hear, and some can choose to play. Barthes writes: "I cannot reproduce the Winter Garden Photograph. It exists only for me. For you, it would be nothing but an indifferent picture, one of the thousand manifestations of the 'ordinary'; . . . at most it would interest your *studium*: period, clothes, photogeny; but in it, for you, no wound" (*Camera Lucida* 73). Does he really feel we'd *get* the point, the maternal *punctum*, with Schumann? That we'd come to know, love, and desire Mme Barthes as well? That we'd even come to grieve her loss? I suppose it's possible, because I could empathize with the wishful thinking behind the feeling. I wish you'd known Linda—and suggest you, too, play *Papillons*.

If you do hear or play the first *Gesang der Frühe* you may wonder why Barthes finds it grievous. Unlike *Funérailles*, which alternates between two lugubrious "tonics" (F minor and an augmented triad built on D-flat), the *Gesang der Frühe* is in D major. Of course, some major chords—or, rather, some compositions written in major—do open to the Other "whose unattainability induces weeping" (Adorno, *Mahler* 26). I, for one, dab my teary eyes whenever I hear the Schumann Fantasie played well, and it's in C major! (Incidentally, Schumann's use of *An die ferne Geliebte*, the Beethoven song cycle, in the Fantasie doesn't represent a *pianistic* cathexis.) What I meant to say is, the *Gesang der Frühe*, which isn't in minor, isn't even very beautiful. Not to me, at any rate. In other words, just as I couldn't hear Barthes's perfectly self-expressive Fantasie as decentered (the dying declaration of my last chapter), I can't understand how the *Gesang der Frühe* "accords both with [his] mother's being and [his] grief at her death." *Papillons*, perhaps—also in major. But not the *Gesang der Frühe*.

I wish you'd known my father as well. Like Linda, he was remarkably intelligent and exceptionally generous, qualities I feel I don't possess, even though I've been told I'm a chip off the old block. Of course, "chip off the old block," unlike "mama's boy," isn't a gay male stereotype. It will do, however, because I can't think of another way to indicate—and to naturalize—something our subculture fails to appreciate: that gay men do love, desire, and identify with their fathers. We *recognize* this cathexis from time to time. Luce Irigaray, for example, incorporates it within the notion of "hom(m)osexuality." But we *marginalize* it, by constantly portraying gay men as effeminate, and even demonize it. "Hom(m)osexuality," after all, isn't a term of endearment. And wasn't it Wilde, a man Sedgwick would describe as gender separatist, who said: "All women become like their mothers. That is their tragedy. No man does. That's his." (*Earnest* 502)

Luckily, one Wildean writer does appreciate the cathexis. J. R. ("Joe") Ackerley, the literary editor who pursued men in uniform and settled for a bitch named Tulip,[8] pursued his (dead) father, Roger, as well. Doggedly, in fact. For not only did Roger turn out to have been a strikingly handsome guardsman, he also turned out to have had "a way of life as shady as my own" (*My Father* 165). Joe was a homosexual, and Roger a bigamist.[9] But whereas Ackerley is well aware of his incestuous desire ("It is true that, studying the photograph of him in uniform, I decided that I would not have picked him up myself; but the picture was said not to do him justice" [*My Father* 199]), he isn't well aware of the man he finds desirable. Roger may have been a sexual outlaw, but he was another kind of sexual outlaw and so remains "lost and unknown" (*My Father* 209)—a semipathetic role model with whom, in retrospect, Joe can't quite identify. Like Barthes, Ackerley can look at a particular image, or for that matter at any image, of his (dead) mother and see her as she really was:

I don't remember ever having had a serious, intimate conversation with my mother in my life; yet when I think of her, as I sometimes do, or look at her photos with that sad face she always put on for photographers, I take much of her psychology to myself. (*My Father* 174)

However, he can't say the same of his father. No photograph "does him justice." No musical score contains "all the possible predicates" from which his being was constituted. And so we're left with the sorry series of metonyms Ackerley himself finds impertinent yet ineradicable:

He was simply my old familiar dad, with his large top-heavy figure, his Elder Statesman look, his Edward VII hat, umbrella, and eternal cigar, his paunch, his moustache, his swivel eye, his jumps and his unsteady gait, his dull commuting, respectable life, his important business, his dreary office pals, and their eternal yarning about chaps putting their hands up girls' frocks (never into boys' flies). (*My Father* 193)

The sexual difference (bigamy/buggery) Ackerley sees as an epistemological "obstacle" needn't be one (*My Father* 108). I feel I knew my own father, whose clothes *I* now wear, and that he knew me, despite our divergent orientations. Speaking as a mama's boy manqué(e), I suspect Ackerley was too fond of his mother, and not too fond of men in uniform, to know his father very well. Unlike his older brother Peter, a "chip of the old block" who died in World War I, Ackerley "was more [his] mother's son than [his] father's" (*My Father* 52, 108). I also suspect, as does Joe, that Roger didn't care to have him overcome that particular "obstacle." For it was only after the death of my own older brother, who like Peter "approximated far closer than I did to the paternal image" (*My Father* 52), that my father realized he'd better "open" up to yet another needy son—a realization that seems to have been intensified, if not occasioned, by my "repeat performance" of the "Aeolian Harp" Etude; that hastened my transformation from "mama's boy" to "chip off the old block"; and that enabled me to hear him "as he really was" in *Funérailles* (F minor), in the Etude (A-flat *major*), and even in the (cathectic?) cadenza Beethoven wrote for Mozart's D minor Piano Concerto. For shortly after Linda died, my father, who wasn't especially musical, heard me perform that concerto and told my mother, "What a beautiful cadenza!" Well, to be honest, what he said was, "What a beautiful *credenza*"—but we'll leave it, and him, at "cadenza."

No, I can't quite leave him, at least, not without mentioning how "beautiful" *he* was. Like Ackerley, I'm rather attracted to my father. He was, to be trite, tall (taller than me), dark (darker than me), and handsome (you get the drift). Not that I imagine "picking him up." I do, however, ogle his early photographs, one in particular (my own "Winter Garden Photograph"), taken *out* of uniform, and now displayed—where else?—on my piano. But displayed, I might add, next to a "Winter Garden Photograph" of my mother, who was equally beautiful and equally attractive. Believe it or not, she's a former "Miss Subways."

Steve, too, was beautiful and attractive. Painfully so. (Think of Virginia Woolf.) He had a "wounded" beauty—only I'm the one who was hurt by it. Whereas the "Winter Garden," or *Dasein*, photographs of my parents fail to "wound" me and so aren't exactly Barthesian, I can't bear to see, or hear, Steve "as he really was"—whatever that means. I never look at his photographs and, even though I think of him when I play *Funérailles*, never touch the ragtime music that would really resurrect him. Steve loved ragtime and played it all the time. If I played it now, if I felt him move me, I'd never stop crying. And so I stick to *Funérailles*, to the "Aeolian Harp" Etude, and to a number of other disembodied and more or less metonymic mementos. If Steve, to me, is Peter Ackerley, he is also Jacob

Flanders, the utterly unrepresentable World War I casualty Virginia Woolf based on Thoby, *her* dead brother. And I am Betty Flanders, who when last heard of was wandering around Jacob's empty room and wondering what to do with, if not quite how to fill, a pair of his "old shoes" (*Jacob's Room* 176).

There is, of course, a word for what I've just described—or, rather, a word for what I've just performed. The word is "abjection," although Julia Kristeva might not think so. Kristeva sees abjection, *Dostoevskian* abjection, as the "collapse of paternal laws." "Is not the world of *The Possessed*," she asks, "a world of fathers [who are] dead?" (*Powers of Horror* 20). But what about the other world of *The Possessed*, the one in which the following colloquy transpires:

> "You're reluctant to meet people and don't like to talk to them very much. Why, then, have you been so candid with me now?"
>
> "With you? Why, [you] look like my brother. Very much. Strikingly so. . . . Dead for seven years. Older brother. Very, very much."
>
> "I suppose he profoundly influenced your way of thinking?"
>
> "N-no, he didn't talk much. Never said anything." (112–13)

And what about the world of *The Waves*, a second threnody for Thoby ("Percival"), in which Woolf ("Neville") gets to express her inner, incestuous bugger. "Percival [is] you," Neville tells one in a series of beautiful young men, "but you are not [Percival]."

You are you. That is what consoles me for [Percival's death]. But if one day you do not come after breakfast, if one day I see you in some looking-glass perhaps looking after another, if the telephone buzzes and buzzes in your empty room, I shall then, after unspeakable anguish, I shall then—for there is no end to the folly of the human heart—seek another, find another, you. (181)

"Steve is you, but you are not Steve." I, too, have mentioned this paradox to more young men than I care to recall. In fact,

I've repeated it so many times that I now find it hard to believe. (Yet another Wildean paradox bites the Barthesian dust.) But it's true, I'm afraid. True enough, at any rate. I still look for the Other in other Others. I still look for Steve in lovers— not "as he really was," but as I wish he'd been (kind, loving, attentive)—and never find him. Perhaps I *should* play ragtime.

Not that Steve is my sole "fantasmatic" Other ("*the* Other"). Nor is he the only Other for whom the expression "as he or she really was" should be glossed "as I wished he or she had been." Contrary to what psychoanalytic theorists would have us believe, some—many? all?—people have multiple fantasmatics.[10] Our identificatory desires are structured by several primal scenes, some (most?) of which occur in early childhood, or that we *think* occur in early childhood, and some of which do not. I love, desire, and identify with my mother, father, and brother. I also love, desire, and identify with Chopin, Liszt, and Schubert. (Not Schumann, not Brahms.) But I really can't claim to *know* them. I "crystallize" these formative beloveds. Like Stendhal, I endow them with qualities they didn't possess and, like Barthes, who failed to appreciate his mother's Brahmsianicity, can't recognize qualities they did.

Another reason I can't claim to know them, individually, is that I cathect them collectively. My father and brother are one person to me, as are Chopin and Liszt—a fantasmatic conflation best exemplified by the fact that I hear all four of them when I listen to *Funérailles*. But not only do I confuse these four figures with one another, I also confuse them with everyone else I've ever loved and lost—a list far more extensive, far less homoerotic, and even far less homosocial, than one might imagine. For not only does this list include every other boyfriend who "abandoned" me (David Abell, first and foremost), it also includes a number of other (dead) young men I've never even met: ancient musical icons (Orpheus, for example), ancient nonmusical icons (Antinous), contemporary musical icons (Dinu Lipatti), and contemporary nonmusical icons (James Dean). The list includes women as well. It includes Linda, of course. But it also includes all the (dead) young women whom Romantic artists, working in a period when "the morbid" was still feminocentric, wanted us to sense, sensualize, and sentimentalize.[11]

In other words, I'm fundamentally "queer." Are you? Although Western culture forces us to see ourselves as either gay or straight, identificatory desires, fully accounted for, often disturb this categorical distinction. Some of you don't need to be told this. When I said that male pianists occupy women's bodies, did you agree? (I was thinking of Clara Schumann at the time.) When I asked, "Am I in love with [Andrews-Koestenbaum-Sedgwick-Chopin]," did you applaud the conflation? When I figured brotherly abjection as motherly and sisterly ("I am Betty Flanders"), did you refuse to write me off as unrigorous? When I referred to Woolf's "inner bugger," did you know what I meant? If you did, you already get the point— that musical necrophilia is indiscriminate because fantasmatic cathexes are indiscriminate. (Or rather, as indiscriminate as culture can allow. How many of us really cathect pets? How many—see my next chapter—cathect children?) If, however, you didn't agree, applaud, refuse, or know, you may need to realize how queer you are and so should think about whom *you* hear when you listen to, or play, music you find sad or beautiful. Chances are your own dead include both men and women. Jacques Derrida's do, and *he* doesn't see himself as particularly gay:

I truly believe that I am singing someone who is dead and that I did not know. I am not singing for the dead (this is the truth according to [Jean] Genet), I am singing a death, *for* a dead man or woman already [*déjà*]. Although since the gender and number remain inaccessible for me I can always play on the plural. (*Post Card* 143)

Musical necrophilia, I should add, isn't the only index of queer self-constitution. "Suture," one's cathexis of male as well as female movie stars, is another. It simply happens to be a particularly remarkable, yet heretofore unremarked, index. Nor is musical necrophilia the only way we know to revive the dead. We talk to their graves. We watch their old films and videos. We also pretend they didn't die. Having never mourned Steve's loss ("abandoned" siblings are closet cases who rarely get to grieve), I for one often wonder, "What if?" What if he hadn't killed himself at 21? What if I'd been spared that trauma? Sometimes I imagine him alive and well, thirty-something, working as an architect, and living with "Richard," the longtime companion who's tried to make Steve kind, loving, and attentive. Yet for a reason I can't quite fathom—you'd have to ask Koestenbaum, who may know me better than I know myself, or Sedgwick, who does know morbidity better than I do—I usually imagine him living a few more years and then dying—like Egorov, but *not* like Liberace—of AIDS. Needless to say, this fantasy involves a deathbed transfiguration, Steve suddenly becoming the brother I'd always wanted. It also involves a consolation very little piano music offers. (And that which does tends to be in major.) I comfort Richard, and let him know that he's still a part of my life and that, just between the two of us, Steve is still a part of our *collective* life.

Egorov. How could I forget him? How could I forget *myself*? Whenever I hear Egorov's impossible and gender-equivocal "voice," I see myself dying of AIDS as well—even though I'm not (yet?) HIV-positive. (I should say "*living* with AIDS," but my image-repertoire is limited to the more or less homophobic equation of gay male sexuality and tragic early death.)

Egorov, who once asked us to remember him "as a pianist with a good sound in the poetical sense of the word, with the music that becomes *my* communication, *my* language," might not have appreciated this solipsistic response. (Note the impossible tense.) He did, however, endorse another one of my positions, that gifted pianists "reincarnate" people they cathect: "I, for example, am an accumulation [of] Horowitz—do not forget him—and Rubinstein and . . . Lipatti" (Mach 2: 60). It's quite possible that a man who was kind enough to share himself (his *living* self) with Lipatti would have been kind enough to share himself (his *dying* self) with me.

Dying, not dead. No matter how potent my morbid cathexes, no matter how (em)pathetic my vicarious investment in equating gay sexuality with tragic death, I can't see myself dead. Can you? We're all supposed to share this blindspot, or *aporia*. It's just common sense (*doxa*). Folk wisdom, for example, tells us if we dream we've died, we *will* die. It's also a focus of deconstructive attention. According to Derrida, for example, "my" death is never, properly speaking, *mine*. "Is my death possible?" he asks. "Can we understand this question? Can I, myself, pose it? Am I allowed to talk about my death?" (*Aporias* 21). Dying, however, is another story altogether, because even though one can't transcend Western metaphysics, one can always "rehearse the break." Which would account for the intriguing and somewhat Heideggerian definition of dying to which Derrida devotes *Aporias*: "awaiting (one another at) the 'limits of truth'" [*Mourir—s'attendre aux "limites de la vérité"*] (*Aporias* 64).[12]

Intriguing, but what does it mean? And how does it relate to musical necrophilia, to the blissful "truth" of the woeful claim, "I am singing a death"? Consider Derrida's own gloss, one he calls the first and last "possibility in this grammatical structure":

When the waiting for *each other* is related to death, to the borders of death, where we wait for each other knowing *a priori*, and absolutely undeniably, that, life always being too short, the one is waiting for the other there, for the one and the other never arrive there together, at this rendezvous (death is ultimately the name of impossible simultaneity and of an impossibility that we know simultaneously, at which we await each other, at the same time, *ama* as one says in Greek: at the same time, simultaneously, we are expecting this anachronism and this contretemps). (*Aporias* 65)

Where does he come up with this stuff? Personally, I suspect he's read Barthes. Consider what Barthes has to say about "I love you," a related grammatical structure:

I hallucinate what is *empirically* impossible: that our two profferings [*I love you*, and *I love you, too*] be made *at the same time*: that one does not follow the other, as if it depended on it. Proffering cannot be double (doubled): only the *single flash* will do, in which two forces join (separate, divided, they would not exceed some ordinary agreement). (*Lover's Discourse* 150)

He's right, of course. We never get what we want when we say "I love you," which is for the beloved to say it to us, and not *back* to us, at the same time. But whence this "proffering"? The "point of departure" for the proffering of "I love you," Barthes writes, is music, because in music, as in the proffering, "desire is [simply] released, as an orgasm." An orgasm, moreover, that "speaks and . . . says: *I-love-you*" (*Lover's Discourse* 149).

   In a word, *Liebestod*. Love and death—for Derrida, for Barthes, for me, and for you as well—merge in the "impossible" orgasmic simultaneity whereby we "arrive there together." Or if not there, here. And if not then, now. Here at my climax, at my limited, and hopelessly Romantic, moment of truth. Yes, *my* truth. ("*My* communication, *my* language.") Not Genet's (*Derrida's* Genet). Not Derrida's—truth as *doxa* we, together,

57

can't quite transcend, truth as a border we can't cross. Not Barthes's—truth as *paradoxa* we, together (for in truth, Barthes is less autoerotic than some suppose), can't quite convey, truth as a moment in time we'll never live to see. But my truth—which, as I ponder what I'm about to say, I feel compelled to call "true *enough*"—falls somewhere, and sometime, in between. In between *doxa* and *paradoxa*. In between time and space, then and there. (I'm at the point when/where these metaphors are of no avail.) And that truth is: I love, desire, identify with, and *miss* Chopin, Liszt, Linda, and everyone else I'd like to be waiting for me when and where I die, even though I know they won't be. After all, I've been waiting for *them*— thanks, in part, to *Funérailles*.

Oh, and one last thing, one final dying declaration. If I *am* dead when you read this, and you fail to hear *me* in *Funérailles*, don't despair. It could be a major undertaking.

Intermezzo

◇ I cathect children—or used to. As a child, I found a
number of youngsters adorable. Steve, of course. Linda's
daughter Carol, too. (My favorite letter from Carol, one
she sent from summer camp, contains the line: "I'm
learning *The Happy Farmer* in order to improve my
sight-reading.") But my strangest crush was on a boy
named David Nish. I used to see, and hear, David in piano competitions our teachers had us enter. He was
blond and slender and usually took first prize. I, neither
blond nor slender, usually took second. We never actually met at these events and so developed what Koestenbaum would call a "complicated, abiding knowledge" of
one another (*Queen's Throat* 241). Years later, we were
introduced by Miss Parker. It was shortly before my
Carnegie Hall "debut." I'd arrived at the studio a few
minutes early to find a breathtakingly handsome young
man, my age, playing rather badly. (Auditioning, really.
I'd stumbled upon their first session.) I can't quite describe my feelings when, having realized who we were,
David and I exchanged a few loaded pleasantries. I do,
however, remember being astonished that a gifted rival
who turned out to be so beautiful hadn't turned out to
be very accomplished. Luckily for him, David was at an
awkward stage—no longer the unself-conscious prodigy
I'd known, not yet the self-conscious virtuoso he'd soon

become. For shortly thereafter, David entered the Juilliard College (I'd attended the Juilliard *Pre*-College), where he developed quite a reputation. A double reputation, in fact. According to my spies, David was known as "Nish the Dish."

CHAPTER 3

~ *Beethoven's Kiss*

Little Tausig plunged into Chopin's A flat
Polonaise with such fire and boldness that
Liszt turned his eagle head, and after a few
bars cried, "I take him!"

Amy Fay, *Music-Study in Germany*

~ "Little" Carl Tausig, when Liszt first heard him, was fourteen years old, the age at which I'd first lost sight of David
Nish. Now, I'm not sure how "little" teenagers really are—or
were—and, oddly enough, neither was Amy Fay.

Liszt loved Tausig as his own child and is always delighted when we
play any of his music. . . . His death was an awful blow to Liszt, for
he used to say, "He will be the inheritor of my playing." I suppose he
thought he would live again in him, for he always says, "Never did
such talent come under my hands." I would have given anything to
have seen them together, for Tausig was a wonderfully clever and cap-
tivating man, and I can imagine he must have fascinated Liszt. They
say he was the naughtiest boy that ever was heard of. (250)

Is Tausig a naughty boy, or a clever man? Who knows.

One thing I do know, however, is that fourteen-year-olds

are sexy. To use a term that doesn't exactly apply to nineteenth-century teenagers, "adolescents" are, by our definition, victimized by raging hormones. A recent entry in the stages of human development, adolescence marks a "vacancy" that happens to be highly eroticized.[1] But not only are adolescents victims of puberty, so too are the men adolescents "captivate"—a newly demonized group to which I, who am captivated by men, do not belong. So, even though I find teenagers relatively unattractive, it's no surprise to me Liszt "took" Tausig. Nor is it any surprise he didn't take him sight unseen. Fay writes:

Tausig's father, who was himself a music-master, took him to Liszt when he was fourteen years old, hoping that Liszt would receive the little marvel as a pupil and protégé. But Liszt would not even hear the boy play. "I have had," he declared positively, "enough of child prodigies. They never come to much." Tausig's father apparently acquiesced in the reply, but while he and Liszt were drinking wine and smoking together, he managed to smuggle the child on to the piano-stool behind Liszt, and signed to him to begin to play. (250–51)

Liszt was struck by Tausig's sound, of course, and probably struck by hearing him play the *Funérailles* Polonaise, but it was only after having "turned his eagle head" toward Tausig that Liszt is claimed, by someone writing in 1873, to have become "fascinated."

The story Fay relates is typical. Many such quasi-sexual myths used to circulate about nineteenth-century child prodigies. But why did they circulate? Why did they tend to concern prodigies who were no longer children? How did they make sense of prodigious talent? And how do we make sense of them today?

By "we," I mean people like me, but I also mean relatively homophobic people. Take the abduction of Muzio Clementi, the world's first piano virtuoso. Here is Arthur Loesser's account:

Peter Beckford, an intellectual, polyglot, Dorsetshire fox hunter, descendant of a fabulously rich family of Jamaica planters, was on a tour in Italy during the 1760's. While in Rome, he became much impressed with the prodigious musical talents of a fourteen-year-old boy: Muzio, the son of a poor silversmith named Clementi. Mr. Beckford induced the father to accept a sizable sum to let him take Muzio to England, there to educate him further and to launch him into the great world. "The celebrated Clementi, whom I bought from his father for seven years," was how Mr. Beckford later referred to the transaction. (222)

Patronage? Perhaps, but other terms—prostitution, pederasty—come to mind as well. Prostitution, because of the purchase. Pederasty, because Peter Beckford was related to William Beckford, the notorious sodomite, a connection Loesser, who fails to mention it, takes for granted. As a matter of fact, the connection has always colored the Clementi myth, and so does go without saying—much to the phobic chagrin of another musicologist. "For some reason," Leon Plantinga writes, "Peter Beckford (1740–1811), the noted fox-hunter, has been persistently confused with his cousin William Beckford (1759–1844), the flamboyant novelist, author of *Vathek*, who lived at Fonthill Abbey in Wiltshire; and this confusion has bedevilled almost all modern accounts of Clementi's life" (4). Flamboyant? Why not say "flaming" and be done with it?[2] And not only does Plantinga refuse to brand the boy with either gay insignia, he also refuses to believe Beckford took *any* substantive interest in Clementi:

Beckford apparently brought Clementi to England simply to provide his new household with minimal, low-cost musical entertainment. Beckford never showed any very striking devotion to music [and] though it is entirely possible that Clementi may on occasion have accompanied Beckford to London, especially after the latter became a Member of Parliament (representing Morpeth) in 1768, there is no record that Beckford ever engaged a teacher for him, or that Clementi or his music figured in any public performance during the Dorset years. (4–5)

To which I respond, if Clementi wasn't studying very hard and wasn't performing very much, what *was* he doing in Dorset? I know what I'd be doing—or trying to do or thinking about doing—with a 27-year-old benefactor, and it, too, goes without saying.

To be honest, the Clementi abduction isn't crucial to this analysis, but not because Beckford wasn't "really" a pederast. Who's to say what he was? And who cares? What matters is what we *think*, or don't think, he was. The abduction isn't crucial because it never captured the public imagination, and so isn't really a "myth." Musical patronage, commonplace in the Age of Enlightenment, failed to attract attention throughout most of the nineteenth century. When the Duke of Lucca, for example, patronized thirteen-year-old Theodore Doehler (1814–56), a Czerny student who became a salon pianist, no one raised an eyebrow. Why, then, do I mention the abduction? For one thing, I'm fascinated by Clementi. We share a birthday, January 23, and hence a ravished zodiacal sign (Aquarius, or Ganymede). For another, the abduction represents a perverse inauguration of piano virtuosity. Think of it as the primal scene that haunts this book. But the most important, and least idiosyncratic, reason I mention it is that the divergent responses of Loesser and Plantinga anticipate and, by anticipating, help situate analogous responses by a second set of musicologists to an actual myth—the myth to which the title *Beethoven's Kiss* refers.

That myth, unlike the one Fay relates, concerns "little" Liszt. But before turning back to Liszt, let's stop to consider myths that concern the pianists with whom he was most closely associated: Thalberg and Chopin. According to Loesser, Thalberg "had been sent to a fine school in Vienna, and there had been brought up with . . . the so-called 'King of Rome,' Napoleon's son by the Empress Marie Louise." The boys became bosom buddies, and when the young "King" sickened and died, Thalberg, disconsolate, did something remarkable, or rather was said to have done something "people enjoyed believing." He "slept for days" in his dead friend's bed, an act of devotion that, for Loesser, "carries just the right flavor of emotional extravagance tinged with obnoxiousness" (371–72). Alan Walker, one of the musicologists invested in "Beethoven's Kiss" (the man has a history of "strange compulsions" concerning Liszt [Perényi 65]), takes a different, and somewhat uncharacteristic, tack. Even though he fails to mention the myth, he tries to trivialize the cathexis the myth betokens: "One of [Thalberg's] fellow students was the Duke of Reichstadt (Napoleon's fourteen-year-old son, the so-called King of Rome), who filled him with military ardour and nearly persuaded him to join the army" (*Liszt* 1: 233).

Why did Thalberg's fans enjoy this myth? Why does Loesser find it extravagant and obnoxious? Why does Walker move it from the boudoir to the battlefield? Various sexual explanations, soon to be articulated, suggest themselves. It should be said, however, that sexual explanations alone won't suffice. Class comes into play as well. The Thalberg myth, for example, probably had to do with a tendency to figure piano virtuosos as aristocrats, a tendency we've yet to outgrow. Sleeping in a king's bed probably confirmed the nobility of a prodigy who was rumored to be the illegitimate son of Prince Moritz Dietrichstein and Baroness von Wetzlar, but who was in fact the legitimate son of Joseph Thalberg and Fortunée Stein.[3] Unfortunately, class analysis, which to my mind isn't always interesting, isn't all-encompassing. It can't account for Thalberg's having slept in a king's *bed*. It can't account for the somewhat phobic reactions of Loesser and Walker, men who, like me, are *very* interested in amassing cultural capital. Nor can it account for *Chopin's* kiss.

We begin, again, with Loesser. According to Loesser, when Chopin heard Gottschalk, then sixteen, perform the E minor Piano Concerto in Pleyel Hall, he leapt to the stage and "kissed the youth in proper Polish-French fashion" (375). Nothing extravagant or obnoxious about that, apparently, because Loesser may have made it up. Most accounts of the incident have Chopin meeting Gottschalk backstage and shaking his hand, an innocuous and almost furtive gesture.[4] Some go so far as to deny there was any such exchange. According to James Huneker, a turn-of-the-century critic, Gottschalk made his Paris debut in 1847, two years after the Pleyel Hall concert, and "shortly before Chopin's death when his interest in music had greatly abated" (52).

Why would Loesser, who claims to find Thalberg's conduct reprehensible, invent this kiss? An aversion to nonmusical necrophilia, coupled with a powerful cathexis of Chopin? I can relate to that. Why does Huneker remove both Chopin and Gottschalk from the scene of the crime? Denial, *tout court*? Or simply distaste for public, or semipublic, displays of homoerotic, or homosocial, affection? (Huneker can imagine Gottschalk playing for Chopin in the privacy of his home, "for he was the first to introduce the Pole's music to America" [52].) I can't relate to that, even though, like anyone who's had to come to terms with homophobia (societal as well as internalized), I understand the denial and the distaste. But if for some reason you can't imagine the various *imaginaires* (cultural as well as individual, nineteenth- as well as twentieth-century, homophobic as well as antihomophobic) responsible for articulating and disarticulating Chopin's kiss, consider the strik-ingly similar story of Beethoven's.

Liszt was eleven, and presumably prepubescent, when he made his Vienna debut in 1822. Beethoven was in town, but failed to attend. Like Liszt in later life, he tried to avoid *Wun-derkinder*. He was also deaf by that time. (The Conversation Books begin in 1818.) Neither of which seems to have prevented him from attending a concert that Liszt gave four months later. And neither of which prevented him from administering the spectacular *Weihekuss*. Or so "they say" (Loesser 182). Just who were, and who are, "they"? Liszt himself, for one, and for mo-tives that probably related to musical, as opposed to class, en-titlement. (He called the kiss an aesthetic "consecration.") The fan for whom seeing was believing, for another. I'm thinking of fans who'd seen "Beethoven Kissing Liszt," a commemora-tive lithograph that, in light of the mutuality of the gesture, may as well be titled "Liszt Kissing Beethoven."[5] They also in-cluded official and semiofficial biographers, such as Anton Schindler, who refers to the incident in two editions of his book on Beethoven (1840 and 1845), and Lina Ramann, who'd consulted Liszt about it. ("What?" Liszt exclaimed when Ra-mann told him people doubted the story. "They want to take my kiss away from me?" [Taylor 10–11].)

Ramann's 1880 version, a chapter titled "The Musical Con-secration," is rather wonderful:

The hall was full to overflowing. When the boy stepped before the public, who looked up at him expectantly, head pressed against head, he perceived Beethoven near the platform, his earnest eye fixed med-itatively. Franz felt a startled joy, but the presence of the deified mas-ter did not bewilder him. He recognized the eye that was directed to-wards him, but his playing only became more fiery and glowing from measure to measure, and his whole being seemed elevated and kin-dled by an invisible power. So it went from passage to passage. The public, taken by surprise, listened in silence, and then gave vent to their feelings all the more loudly and vehemently.

And when Franz had finished and surpassed all expectation his improvisation of a supposed theme, he scarcely knew what was going on; he was as in a dream. The audience crowded and pressed around him, and *Beethoven had hastily mounted the platform and kissed him.* (74–75)[6]

Unfortunately, Ramann doesn't indicate how many times Beethoven kissed Liszt. Nor does she indicate where he kissed him. Where on Liszt's body, that is. The fact that Beethoven kissed him on a "platform" isn't very remarkable, especially in view of the fact that the lithograph doesn't show one. These are, in fact, questions of considerable importance that, when answered, speak to myth makers' fantasies. (I include myself in that group.) The lithographer, who has the two in preliminary suspended animation, can't seem to decide. (They look to me as if they're about to French kiss.) Nor can he show them doing anything repeatedly. However, a second Liszt biographer, writing in 1925, has other ideas:

The hall was crowded, and Franz, on coming on the platform, found himself confronted with the massive leonine figure of the great composer seated in the front row. Far from being agitated by the apparition, he seemed inspired to higher flights than heretofore. He played [the Hummel] concerto with the utmost brilliancy, and concluded, as was customary, with a "Fantasia" or improvisation on themes given by the audience—not, to his disappointment, by Beethoven. The hearers were frantic in their demonstrations of delight, in which Beethoven himself could not refrain from joining. Ascending the steps of the platform, he folded the boy in his arms and kissed him repeatedly, accompanied by the wild cheers of the whole assembly. (Corder 13–14)

Now that's more like it—or would be if I had a thing for eleven-year-olds. But it's too much for Harold Schonberg, who'd prefer to have Beethoven kissing Liszt, if at all, "on the forehead" and in private.

According to Schonberg, "present-day scholars are inclined to doubt" the myth (*Great Pianists* 163–64). Well, not Walker. Maybe things would be different if Perényi—*Baroness* Perényi —had ever taken him to task for an intimation of his "strange" investment in the *Weihekuss*, but as things stand, Walker is standing by this particular "compulsion." Or, rather, he's standing by the story that the kiss occurred on the forehead and in Beethoven's home, a version of the myth I'd call domesticated, but some, including the rival Lisztomaniac with whom Walker is most closely associated, would still call disreputable. Walker cites three sources. The Conversation Books, he claims, corroborate the fact that a private meeting took place. An 1862 letter to the Grand Duke of Weimar, in which Liszt recalls Beethoven having "consecrated [his] brow with a kiss" but fails to recall the concert, corroborates the fact that the meeting was unusually intimate (*Liszt* 1: 84).[7] And an oral account Liszt gave to a student named Ilka Horowitz-Barnay in 1875 represents proof beyond a reasonable doubt. Walker reproduces the account in its entirety and, due in part to my own morbid fascination, so will I:

"I was about eleven years of age when my venerated teacher Czerny took me to Beethoven. He had told the latter about me a long time before, and had begged him to listen to me play sometime. Yet Beethoven had such a repugnance to infant prodigies that he had always violently objected to receiving me. Finally, however, he allowed himself to be persuaded by the indefatigable Czerny, and in the end cried impatiently: 'In God's name, then, bring me the young Turk!' It was ten o'clock in the morning when we entered the two small rooms in the Schwarzpanier house which Beethoven occupied, I somewhat shyly, Czerny amiably encouraging me. Beethoven was working at a long, narrow table by the window. He looked gloomily at us for a time, said a few brief words to Czerny, and remained silent when my kind teacher beckoned me to the piano. I first played a short piece by Ries. When I had finished, Beethoven asked me whether I could play a Bach fugue. I chose the C-minor Fugue from the Well-Tempered Clavier. 'And could you also transpose the fugue at once into another key?' Beethoven asked me. Fortunately I was able to so. After my closing chord I glanced up. The great master's darkly glowing gaze lay piercingly upon me. Yet suddenly a gentle smile passed over his gloomy features, and Beethoven came quite close to me, stooped down, put his hand on my head, and stroked my hair several times. 'A devil of a fellow,' he whispered, 'a regular young Turk!' Suddenly I felt quite brave. 'May I play something of yours now?' I boldly asked. Beethoven smiled and nodded. I played the first movement of the C-major Concerto. When I had concluded Beethoven caught hold of me with both hands, kissed me on the forehead, and said gently: 'Go! You are one of the fortunate ones! For you will give joy and happiness to many other people! There is nothing better or finer!'" Liszt told the preceding in a tone of deepest emotion, with tears in his eyes, and a warm note of happiness sounded in the simple tale. For a brief space he was quiet, and then he said: "This event in my life has remained my greatest pride—the palladium of my whole career as an artist. I tell it but very seldom and—only to good friends!" (Walker, *Liszt* 1: 83–84)[8]

Allan Keiler, a would-be Liszt biographer who's had his thunder stolen by Alan Walker, claims to understand why Liszt believed this sordid little tale, but can't claim to understand why Walker does. Keiler's take on Liszt is pseudo-Freudian. Having lost a father just when his "adolescence was coming to a close, at a time when the father's affirmation of his son's readiness for independent self-realization is most critical, an affirmation often conferred by a ritual act of blessing," Liszt constructed a "family romance . . . around the figure of Beethoven"—a "wish-fulfilling" construction that, given Beethoven's reluctance to see him, either in public or in private, required more than a little mental labor. It required, that is,

"denial" (of Beethoven's lack of interest) as well as "idealiza-
tion" (of his own disappointing parent) and "displacement"
("of paternal identification onto the figure of Beethoven").
This, we're told, is all very "complicated" ("Liszt and Beethoven" 123; "Liszt Research" 396). But what about his take on
Walker? Setting aside for the moment Keiler's problematic use
of "adolescence" and turning to his treatment of the three
sources, how might that take be described?

For Keiler, the Conversation Books, upon close inspection,
invite one of two interpretations: either Beethoven never saw
Liszt, or their one encounter was "brief and unfriendly" ("Liszt
Research" 391). The letter to the Grand Duke, "the only account of the *Weihekuss* given directly by Liszt himself" ("Liszt
and Beethoven" 127), proves the kiss to have been fantasmatic,
because it situates Liszt's recollection within a "dreamlike" impression of having been visited by several musical ghosts (Al-
legri, Mozart, and Beethoven himself) in the Sistine Chapel.
However, much to Liszt's credit, the letter also indicates oedi-
pal improvement, because in it one finds "the passive infan-
tilism of his youthful belief in the paternal image symbolized
in the *Weihekuss* . . . replaced by a more mature and realistic
acceptance of paternal obligation and love."[9] The Horowitz-
Barnay account is "virtually impossible to believe" ("Liszt Research" 389).[10] The contents alone "conflict with the evidence
of the Conversation Books," some of which Walker himself
mentions. And even on its own terms, "it is improbable and
calculated for effect. No actual meeting would have produced
so dramatic a transformation in Beethoven's response, even
if he could have heard anything. The detail is too intentionally precise for an account recollected after half a century, and
the narrative buildup corresponds too obviously to the traditional picture of Beethoven's moodiness and irascibility" ("Liszt

Research" 389–90). This traditional picture, moreover, is part of an even bigger one, because the Horowitz-Barnay account features several familiar aspects of the legend: the difficulty of getting Beethoven to Liszt's concert ("here transformed into [his] suspicious willingness to hear Liszt play"); the remarkable effect Liszt has on Beethoven; "the actual gesture of fatherly benediction"; Beethoven's "predilection" [sic] about Liszt's future; and the "significance" for Liszt thereof ("Liszt and Beethoven" 126). (I find the slippage between Beethoven's "prediction" and Keiler's—unspeakable?—"predilection" equally significant.)

It's hard to know where to begin unpacking. Fortunately, Keiler himself provides several symptomatic directions. Whereas Keiler is complicated and knowledgeable, Walker is "simple" and "naive" ("Liszt and Beethoven" 123). Whereas Keiler is fair-minded and profound, Walker is "one-sided and superficial" ("Liszt Research" 378). Whereas Keiler has a healthy appreciation for historical accuracy, Walker has "an almost pathological predilection" for "gossipy" storytelling ("Liszt Research" 377). (There's that "predilection" again.) Whereas Keiler, moreover, has a "sympathetic understanding" of Marie d'Agoult (Liszt's mistress), Walker, who according to Keiler finds her "horrifying," has a misogynistic one ("Liszt Research" 401, 399). So now we know to whom those other undesirable attributes ("infantile," "passive," "unrealistic"), the ones Keiler uses to predicate young Liszt, really apply. They apply to Walker. And now we know why Beethoven was so "unfriendly." "Little" Liszt probably seemed a lot like Walker. In other words, why doesn't Keiler just say "flaming" and be done with it? Walker, we're to believe, is stereotypically gay (naive, superficial, pathological, gossipy, misogynist, infantile, passive, unrealistic) in ways that for Keiler, who sees the stereotypicality (doxicality) of the Horowitz-Barnay account as one measure of *its* unreliability, discredit anything the man has to say. Given that his own account of the *Weihekuss* is stereotypically psychoanalytic, not to mention incredibly *un*complicated, Keiler's pseudo-Barthesian paradoxicality isn't especially profound. Nor is it especially self-reflexive. But given the possibility that Keiler, too, is gay—I'm just imagining, Alan and Allan, and neither know nor care what you "really" are—it is especially perverse.

Unlike Keiler, I don't know why Liszt "really" believed the myth. I do know, however, that I can't credit his "family romance." Neither the *Weihekuss* itself nor the other startling gesture to which Horowitz-Barnay refers, the pre-concerto hair fondling, seems to me to be especially, or exclusively, fatherly. I can't recall my own father kissing me or playing with my hair—he was probably too concerned with what either would mean about him and do to me—and so must imagine Liszt, even though nineteenth-century parents had fewer such scruples, construing these gestures, if he did construe them as anything other than signs of musical entitlement, as somewhat sexual. The sexual connotation, or possible sexual connotation, of a kiss—even on the forehead—goes without saying. And, given that connotation, the business with the hair comes to seem like a form of foreplay. Anyway, who's to say "little" Liszt wasn't a little queer? Who's to say he didn't desire either "father"? Who's to say he didn't cathect Beethoven? And who's to say he didn't envision this cathexis as reciprocal? Loving a father, even a supplemental father, may give rise to more than one wish-fulfilment. Just ask J. R. Ackerley.

Nor do I know why Walker "really" believes in the *Weihekuss*. However, assuming he's attracted to the myth because it's somewhat sordid—and setting aside for the moment why

he shouldn't see it in that light—I can imagine why he'd prefer the domesticated version. Walker restages the *Weihekuss*
as a closet drama for the same reason Huneker has Gottschalk
play in Chopin's home. Both writers embrace the familiar (het-
erocentric, phallocentric) logic that situates heterosexuality
and masculinity in the public sphere and homosexuality and
femininity in the private. Or at least they seem to embrace it.
For by *publicizing* these purportedly private quasi-sexual encounters, are they not in fact undermining this logic? They
also embrace, or at least flirt with, the familiar presumption
that private encounters are far more sexual than public. It's so
much easier to envision Beethoven and Liszt getting it together
"in the Schwarzpanier house" than doing so in the Redou-
tensalle. Or it would be if Beethoven had been living there at
the time.[11]

Why *shouldn't* Walker see the kiss as sordid? Because he's
not supposed to find teenage boys, let alone eleven-year-old
boys, sexually attractive. Contemporary men are more prone
to homosexual panic, and hence to homophobia, than were
nineteenth-century counterparts. We're also more prone to a
panic and fear for which we have no such terminology. "Child-
loving," to borrow James Kincaid's expression, makes us very,
very anxious. The sense that our loving feelings for youngsters are going too far, or too far in the wrong direction, makes
us, to use a number of psychoanalytic stereotypes, deny the
feelings, repress their physical expression, and project them
onto "perverted" and "seductive" bogeymen. It's easy to see
this is so where "innocent" children are concerned. It's easy
to see, in other words, that Walker is more comfortable having Beethoven kiss Liszt on the forehead, as any father might
do without engaging in conduct unbecoming, than he would
be if the kiss had been somewhat French. It's not so easy to

see this is so where adolescents are concerned, especially the older and sexier they get. But it's still the case. Even though we distinguish "adolescence" from childhood and adulthood, we're compelled—by binaristic thinking, by an aversion to Barthesian "third terms"—to categorize adolescents as either children or adults. Usually, when push comes to shove, it's children. We do "let" them date, drive, and shop. (How cute!) But we rarely try teenage boys as adults, even though we know they're criminals. We rarely give them condoms, even though we know they're sexually active. And we never give them condoms when they're involved with older men.

Why are we more uptight than Romantics and Victorians? As many Foucauldians have argued, nineteenth-century thinkers didn't exactly polarize heterosexuality and homosexuality. We alone can take credit for doing that. And although they did polarize childhood and adulthood, they didn't exactly equate (prepubescent) "child-loving" with child molesting. Once again, we alone, who love to torture daycare providers, can take credit for that. Nor did nineteenth-century thinkers tend to categorize teenagers as children. Not having "adolescence" to fall back on, they categorized, and to a certain extent sexualized, teenagers as adults. Very young women were used by, and very young men employed by, considerably older men. Put it all together, and you'll begin to see why these myths circulated about piano prodigies. Anyone could love a child without being called a menace to society. And anyone could homoeroticize and/or homosocialize—the distinction hasn't always been crucial—a teenage boy without being called a pederast. Could it be that Keiler is putting it together, that he's thinking about these forms of licentiousness and not about a more conventional notion of the period (as sentimental, as spiritual) when, hurling one final, crypto-gay epithet, he describes Walker as "Romantic" ("Liszt and Beethoven" 123)? Probably not, but given the possibility that Walker does see the *Weihekuss* as sordid, he might as well be.

Of course, the myths don't concern any old children. They concern *prodigies*. How might this be accounted for? And does it help explain the circulation? Prodigies display uncanny, unself-conscious, and premature musical ability. They play things mere mortals take years and years to master, if at all, and hence seem more adultlike than others their own age. Consider how one newspaper reported Liszt's Vienna debut:

A young virtuoso has, as it were, fallen from the clouds, and compels us to the highest admiration. The performance of this boy, for his age, borders on the incredible, and one is tempted to doubt any physical impossibility when one hears the young giant, with unabated force, thunder out Hummel's composition, so difficult and fatiguing, especially in the last movement. [It was especially] fine to see the little Hercules unite Beethoven's andante from the Symphony in A and the theme of the cantilena from Rossini's *Zelmira*, and knead them, so to speak, into one paste. *Est deus in nobis!*[12]

Eleven-year-old Liszt is a "giant," a "Hercules," a god one sees as well as hears. Or if not a god, a Paganini-like demon. ("A devil of a fellow," according to the Horowitz-Barnay Beethoven.) And if the prodigies happened to be teenagers, they seemed even more adultlike. Fay's Tausig, age fourteen, was a "clever man."

No wonder, re-viewing "Beethoven Kissing Liszt," we find the two clasping one another. Given nineteenth-century licentiousness, and given the prodigious talent that raised Liszt to Beethoven's level, they can afford to make a spectacle of themselves. They can afford to express, in public, their reciprocal and nonhierarchical cathexes. Just look at them. Don't they seem to say "I love you" at the same point in time? Hasn't the lithographer "hallucinated what is *empirically* impossible"—the mutual "proffering" Barthes (*Lover's Discourse* 150) would love to see (and hear)? Not that I'd call the lithograph a *Liebestod*, even though Beethoven did die shortly thereafter. Nor would I call it a moment of truth. For some reason— whether because I can't admit Walker's hearsay evidence (if only Liszt's letter to the Grand Duke were a hearsay exception—a dying declaration, perhaps) or because I've been led to distrust the pederastic predilection such admission has come to represent—I simply don't believe the *Weihekuss* really happened. But I would call the lithograph a mutual, musical orgasm, the kind that "speaks and . . . says: *I-love-you*" (*Lover's Discourse* 149). Ramann, it seems, couldn't imagine this bilateral extreme. However, the unmistakably blissful note with which she concludes "The Musical Consecration," one I've already had her sound—"[Liszt] was as in a dream, [the audience] crowded and pressed around him, and *Beethoven had hastily mounted the platform and kissed him*"—does envision a unilateral one. It does, that is, represent the *Weihekuss* as an orgasmic moment for Liszt alone.

I, too, am about to climax, on a newfangled but silent keyboard, and will do so with the help of a musical Modernist who was brave enough to anatomize contemporary neoclassical pederasty ("active" *erastes* / "passive" *eromenos*). Thomas Mann, shortly before having written *Der Tod in Venedig* (1911) and shortly after the fearsome invention of "homosexuality," wrote a story called "Das Wunderkind" (1903). In it, a piano prodigy, an eight-year-old Greek boy who looks a little older, claims to be a little younger, and acts like a little girl, stimulates himself, his impresario, and, by extension, much of his public. ("He looked as though he were nine years old but was

really eight and given out for seven" ["Wunderkind" 340].)
Whenever Bibi Saccellaphylaccas performs, he experiences a
"private pleasure" Mann describes as a "prickling delight" and
"secret shudder of bliss" (340–41). Audience members are
aroused as well. Male members, that is. Women attending his
performance have a hard time conceiving Bibi sexually. One
girl, for example, thinks to herself: "What is it he is playing?
He plays passion, yet he is a child. If he kissed me it would be
as though my little brother kissed me—no kiss at all" (345).
The impresario, however, reenacts the *Weihekuss*. Taking his
cue, or so it would appear, from Horowitz-Barnay, he mounts
the stage, hangs a laurel wreath around Bibi's neck, "tenderly
strokes the black hair—and suddenly as though overcome . . .
bends down and gives the prodigy a kiss, a resounding kiss,
square on the mouth." The kiss "runs through the crowd like
a nervous shudder," the men go wild, and their storm of applause turns into a "hurricane" (346).

Unbelievable, isn't it? But think about how long ago this
was written. "The Wunderkind" and *Death in Venice* reflect
an epistemic shift in the history of sexuality. The earlier story
was meant for men who still enjoyed loving children in general and child prodigies in particular. If Bibi is supposed to be
seven (instead of eight), he seems all the more prodigious. If
he's supposed to be prodigious, he seems all the more adult.
(One critic thinks Bibi's "already quite complete, an artist *par
excellence*" ["Wunderkind" 346].) If he's supposed to be adult,
he seems all the more sexual. Why, then, isn't Bibi supposed
to be a teenager? Why isn't he "takeable" little Tausig's age
(fourteen)? Because the feminine passivity demanded by the
Dorian mode—the mode of *Death in Venice* as well (Tadzio
constantly recalls Greek sculpture)—had yet to be associated
with (childlike) "adolescence." It was, however, so associated

by the time Tadzio—also fourteen, but *un*takeable—rolled around. In other words, readers who cared to see themselves as impresarios, and *not* as doting, dispassionate fathers, could sit back, relax, and think about stroking Bibi's hair—*clearly* a form of foreplay—and kissing him on the mouth. And if a "nervous shudder" were to run through *them*—why, nothing could be more normal. It happens to everyone, according to Romantic Mann.

Or used to. I, for one, don't care to see myself as the impresario. In fact, the only "nervous shudder" I've had while writing this chapter is unrelated to Tausig, Clementi, Thalberg, Gottschalk, Liszt, and "Saccellaphylaccas." Having had the frightening realization that David Nish might be dead, and hence belong in "Funérailles," I consulted directory assistance and dialed the David Nish who lives in Greenwich Village. Much to my relief, the voice on his answering machine sounded somewhat familiar. (I left no message, of course, but hope this chapter, unlike Derrida's postcard, will arrive at that original destination.) And much to my surprise, my heart was racing.

What was I thinking? Was I remembering the first time we'd lost sight of one another—David at fourteen? Was I remembering the last—David at eighteen? Or was I remembering the *two* of us at seven, eight, or nine? Bibi's age.

Intermezzo

∾ The morning after my "gay debut," David Abell announced: "You've just slept with someone who slept with someone who slept with someone who slept with someone who slept with *Liszt*!" "So?" I replied, "I *study* with someone who studied with someone who studied with someone who studied with Liszt." It was an odd thing for him to say. He'd traced his sexual competence, as well as his homosexual predilection, to a musical master known to be a ladies' man. It was also an odd thing for me to say. I'd equated "sleeping with" and "studying with," but also discriminated between the two. I'd won by having fewer of the same kind of intermediaries, but also won by having engaged in a better kind of intercourse.

CHAPTER 4

∾ *The Sexual Virtuoso*

I don't know if [Andras Schiff] likes my playing. I don't think I'm his type.

Vladimir Horowitz, quoted in David Dubal,
Evenings with Horowitz

∾ Up until a year ago, when I discovered it was also Clementi's birthday, I'd always thought of January 23 as the day
Anna Pavlova died. Why recall this coincidence (my birthday,
her death day)? Because I dreamt of being a ballerina long before I ever dreamt of being a virtuoso. One of my earliest im-
pressions is of Pavlova, on film, dancing *The Dying Swan*. The
suture involved—not to mention the terpsichorean necrophilia—was, of course, fundamentally queer. I was a four-year-
old boy who saw himself as a forty-year-old woman. It was
seamless as well. All of a sudden, I *was* Pavlova, and so had
my brother play Saint-Saëns's *The Swan* over and over again,
perfecting my own dying swan as he did so. Bob, to his credit,
never ridiculed the routine. My parents, however, having had
us perform for them, did. Unaware of my incompetence (I

didn't know I needed lessons) as well as of my abnormality (I didn't know I was too young, and too male, for the part), I was stunned by their laughter, but pretended I'd been in on the joke all along. Needless to say, I retired from that particular stage and began to worry about other ways my body would betray me.

No wonder I've never really liked *The Red Shoes* (1948). (I was nine the first time I saw it.) Or, more to the point, no wonder I've never really seen myself as Moira Shearer—even though, like Pavlova, she danced herself to death and even though *The Red Shoes* is less stagy and more sophisticated than *The Dying Swan* (1924), a flick that merely situates viewers as live audience members. A "women's film," *The Red Shoes* would have me see Shearer, and hence station myself, as a straight female subject who also happens to be an object of the straight male gaze. It would also have me be the straight male subject of the gaze. But I'm not too queer to make these leaps. For one thing, I'm gullible. I still find movies like *The Red Shoes* real and so still find myself in them. For another, I'm morbid. I still enjoy the vicarious thrill of imagining I'm Bette Davis in *Dark Victory* or Joan Crawford in *What Ever Happened to Baby Jane?* The reason I don't see myself as Shearer, the reason I can't make that particular leap, is that she's a better ballerina than I could hope to be. In other words, she's too damn perfect. And so the queer suture involved here is far less seamless than it would be, or would have been, had I never danced at all.

Notice I haven't said "cathexis." Love, desire, and identification aren't always coterminous. I wanted to be Pavlova, even though I don't recall having desired her. I do, however, recall having desired Shearer, even though I couldn't see myself in her toe shoes. Masters (parental, pedagogical, professional) can act as role models—on occasion. And mastery (athletic, intellectual, musical) can act as an aphrodisiac—on occasion. But feelings of inferiority, especially ones based on experience, can prevent us from identifying with masters we desire. I've always found Misha Dichter, a powerful pianist, sexy. He's *my* type. But I've yet to introject him as an ego ideal. After all, he's no Chopin.

I was nine when I first fell for Dichter. I was at a youth concert, and Dichter was playing a Brahms Concerto under Michael Tilson Thomas. (I knew even then, Bob having told me, that Thomas had had an affair with Leonard Bernstein.) But what if I hadn't already known I'd never be a great pianist? And what if I'd had a slightly different—less performative but equally pianistic—introduction to sexual virtuosity? In other words, what if, instead of *The Red Shoes*, I'd been taken to see *Letter from an Unknown Woman*, another women's film made in 1948. (Yes, it's a strange rhetorical turn, but Koestenbaum— "Chopin . . . remind[s] me of movies I haven't seen" ["Piano Life" ll. 73–74]—would appreciate it.)

Letter from an Unknown Woman, like a number of films by Max Ophuls, takes us to turn-of-the-century Vienna—a time and place we've already visited. (Think of the *Weihekuss* and of the epistemic shift that transformed the *Weihekuss*.) In it, Lisa Berndle (Joan Fontaine) is seduced and abandoned by Stefan Brand (Louis Jourdan), a profligate pianist who plays a lot of Liszt, *Un Sospiro* (a Concert Etude) in particular. Lisa bears his son, carries a torch, marries a man she doesn't love, runs into Stefan at the opera, stirs things up again, realizes he doesn't remember her, and decides to leave well enough alone. Unfortunately, the movie won't leave well enough alone. Lisa loses her son, contracts the disease that killed him, and prompts her husband to challenge Stefan to a duel. The pianist has no intention of fighting ("Honor," he tells his valet, "is a luxury only gentlemen can afford" [Wexman 32]), but changes his mind after reading the "peculiarly potent" explanation Lisa dies writing. "By the time you read this letter," her haunting voice-over begins, "I may be dead" (35).

Who says twentieth-century sentimentality is phallocentric? Sedgwick. But it's both feminocentric and phallocentric. Lisa is a pathetic spectacle, a beautiful dead body men are meant to desire and women are meant to be. According to the April 1948 *Variety* review, she has "femme appeal" (Wexman 215). (Little did the reviewer realize the extent of Lisa's "femme appeal"—that *women* find her attractive, and *men* find themselves in her place.) Stefan, who's about to be killed in the duel, is a pathetic spectacle as well. He's a beautiful *dying* body women are meant to desire. Why else cast Jourdan? But he *isn't* someone men are meant to be. For one thing, Stefan is somewhat womanish. For another, he's all washed up. Virtuosos may be far more phallic than amateurs, but the sexual virtuosity that feminizes Stefan—according to one critic, he's "a male Lola Montez" (Wexman 234)—diminishes his musical virtuosity as well. (Lola Montez is the eponymous heroine of Ophuls's final film.) In the words of a catty coterie Lisa overhears at the opera:

> WOMAN: Look, isn't that Stefan Brand?
> FIRST MAN: He returned last week.
> SECOND MAN: A concert tour?
> WOMAN: Pleasure trip most likely.
> SECOND MAN: The way he's burning himself up it's a wonder he's still alive. Ten years ago he showed great promise. Too bad. With that talent, he could have been a great pianist.
> FIRST MAN: Perhaps talent is not enough.
> WOMAN: Perhaps he has too many talents. (Wexman 107–8)

Oddly enough, the ideology that compels Ophuls to castrate Stefan, one I'll scrutinize, fails to inflect the 1922 novella

on which *Letter from an Unknown Woman* is based. Stefan
Zweig's text concerns a *successful* artist—a writer, not a pianist—who isn't about to die, who isn't effeminate, and whose
sexual expenditure doesn't reduce his cultural capital. (Un-
surprisingly, Ophuls's producer, John Houseman, and screen-
writer, Howard Koch, both came to believe that the novella is
about a musician.)[1] "Somehow you are two people in one,"
the anonymous correspondant tells the anonymous novelist,
"a passionate, happy-go-lucky young man given over to pleasure and adventure, and at the same time as far as your writing is concerned, a relentless, serious, responsible, extremely
well-read and educated man" (Wexman 161). However, neither Stefan's effeminacy nor the professional distress that both
produces and is produced by that effeminacy—a distress his
recognition of Lisa and reciprocation of the conjugal love she
proffers would have alleviated—makes him *totally* unattractive. Lisa, who can recall his youthful bravura, still finds Stefan sexy. As do I, who, nowadays, am sutured into Lisa's subject position (the "salvific victim") as readily as Stefan is sutured into the position Lisa creates for him (the "honorable
gentleman"). It helps, of course, that Stefan is played by an actor I find sexy. I don't find Orson Welles attractive, even as
Jane Eyre's (Fontaine's) brooding master. (But what if Roch-
ester played the piano?) And not everyone shares my taste.
Houseman, in retrospect, claimed casting Jourdan may have
been a mistake: "Louis Jourdan was French, in his midtwen-
ties, dark, slender, with regular features and flashing eyes. He
seemed too good to be true. As it turned out he had everything, except sex—which for American audiences meant he
lacked the combination of glandular and muscular attraction
that makes for a sense of danger and therefore brings star-
dom" (Wexman 193). Presumably, however, someone on the

set—maybe even Houseman himself—thought Jourdan was sexy enough to play *young* Stefan. Could it be that many (male) Americans couldn't discriminate between Jourdan and the castrated, and therefore unsexy, older pianist he came to play?

Would I, at nine, have found Jourdan as desirable as Dichter? It's hard to say. For one thing, I had yet to see myself as a *salvific* victim. For another, I don't recall having loved the older Jourdan of *Gigi*, which I had seen at that age. But I would have identified with him. Had I not had "pianist envy," I would have introjected youthful, brilliant Stefan as an ego ideal. And having had pianist envy, I would have done what I still do. I would have empathized with Stefan's terminal disability. Nor would I have been the only proto-gay child, the only femme-bryo, to have done so. To quote the score card of an unknown audience member—I'll call him "Kevin"—who attended the film's Pasadena preview, a card Ophuls claimed to find funny:

> How did you find the film? . . . Terrific.
> Was the story clear? . . . Crystal clear.
> And the casting? . . . Brilliant.
> The music? . . . Beautiful.
> What changes in the cast would you suggest? . . . It
>   was perfect.
> What do you think of the theme? . . . Marvellous.
> Could you identify with the characters? . . . Ab-
>   solutely.
> Will you recommend this film to your friends? . . .
>   Certainly.
> Sex? . . . Male.
> Age? . . . Nine years. (Rivette and Truffaut 22)

"Kevin's" queer identification, with Lisa as well as Stefan, young Lisa as well as old Lisa, and young Stefan as well as old Stefan, is "absolute." His suture is seamless, which shouldn't have amused the director. Ophuls should have read Kevin's reaction as a sign of the film's sophistication and widespread femme appeal. Perhaps he did, but couldn't say so.

Suture is, in fact, the right word for my reaction to *The Dying Swan*. It's also the word for my reaction to the Dichter concert. Film technology—fetishistic lighting, shot/reverse-shot sequencing, etc.—may be more sophisticated than stage technology, but the interpellations they help establish are almost identical. My partial cathexis of Dichter way back when, a cathexis which may or may not have been mediated by Thomas, and my current partial cathexis of Jourdan, which *is* mediated by Fontaine, are otherwise analogous. Our identificatory and erotic investments in performers (actors, instrumentalists, vocalists) resemble—and, historically speaking, prefigure—our investments in movie stars. Any number of conventional texts indicate this resemblance, including *Letter from an Unknown Woman*. No one loves and desires Stefan more than Lisa, who heard him live. A number of unconventional texts indicate this resemblance as well, including a pornographic novel attributed to Oscar Wilde.

René Teleny, the eponymous hero of the Wilde novel, is a brilliant pianist who has an interesting effect on male audience members. The narrator, for example, is "spellbound" by Teleny's rendition of a Lisztian rhapsody,[2] wonders whether he's reacting to "the composition, the execution, or the player himself," and has a vision that foreshadows their final fatal union. (The novel ends with a *Liebestod*.)[3] But things get out of hand—or taken in hand, depending on your point of view:

Then—in the very midst of my vision—the pianist turned his head and cast one long, lingering, slumberous look at me, and our glances met. . . . That thrilling longing I had felt grew more and more intense, the craving so insatiable that it was changed to pain; the burning fire had now been fanned to a mighty flame, and my whole body was convulsed and writhed with mad desire. My lips were parched, I gasped for breath; my joints were stiff, my veins were swollen, yet I sat still, like all the crowd around me. But suddenly a heavy hand seemed to be laid upon my lap, something was hent and clasped and grasped, which made me faint with lust. The hand was moved up and down, slowly at first, then fast and faster it went in rhythm with the song. My brain began to reel as throughout every vein a burning lava coursed, and then, some drops even gushed out—I panted—

All at once the pianist finished his piece with a crash amidst the thundering applause of the whole theatre. . . . I was powerless to applaud; I sat there dumb, motionless, nerveless, exhausted. My eyes were fixed upon the artist who stood there bowing listlessly, scornfully; while his own glances full of "eager and impassioned tenderness," seemed to be seeking mine and mine alone. What a feeling of exultation within me! But could he love me, and me only? (*Teleny* 26–27)

Command Performance (1992), a porn video made a hundred years after *Teleny*, is another such text. In it, B. J. Slater hears multi-talented Chuck Hunter perform Rachmaninov's C-sharp minor Prélude—a piece that, according to Adorno, enables "infantile" amateurs to imitate "virtuosi who have been swotting up their Liszt"[4]—and starts to fantasize. To quote the promotional brochure:

The passion of the pianist, each key responding to the touch of the virtuoso. The music rises, then retreats back—faster then slower, softer then louder. The beautiful young man [Slater] has succumbed to the force of the music and of his wild, inflamed lover [Hunter]. They're taken further and further into the realm of wild sensual passions . . . The music grows with intensity, ever increasing in tempo and excitement . . . the two men reach for a climax . . . the music finds its final release . . . the men heave and groan with unrelenting zeal. (Ellipses in original)

Whoever wrote this, however, didn't do his homework—or the right kind of homework. The music neither grows with intensity nor increases in excitement. It becomes lis[z]tless long before the sexual climax, which, as in *Teleny*, does coincide with the applause. Chuck begins with Rachmaninov, but proceeds to Debussy (*Clair de lune*) and Satie (the first *Gymnopédie*).

Clearly, stagy suture hasn't changed very much. Young concert pianists, after all, still stimulate gay men. But the two unconventional texts are dissimilar. For one thing, even though both correlate musical and sexual climax, and so can be said to feature love-deaths, no one really dies in *Command Performance*, which might mean it's less internally homophobic than *Teleny*. For another, the suture contained within and peddled by the video is relatively partial. Like a lot of contemporary pornography, *Command Performance* is unromantic. B. J., hearing Chuck play, lies back and lifts his heels, but doesn't fall head over heels.[5] Nor do we. The video is nonidentificatory as well. B. J. doesn't see himself as Chuck, even though he doesn't have pianist envy and even though the Prélude "owes its popularity to listeners who identify with the performer" (Adorno, *Quasi una Fantasia* 38). ("They know they could do it just as well," says Adorno. "The sombre mood of destruction which the Slav idiom of the piece simultaneously threatens and glorifies arouses in every listener the certainty that in the foreboding gloom he too could easily smash the piano to pieces" [38, 39].) Wilde's narrator, however, does love, and does see himself as, Teleny. And the feeling, unlike Lisa's, is mutual. "You are . . . my *Doppelgänger*," the pianist tells him, "[my] *alter ego*" (*Teleny* 125).

Not that gay men alone find pianists stimulating. Liszt, as is well known, enthralled thousands of women, many of whom managed to sleep with him. Gottschalk wowed women as well. So did Paderewski. The point is, both men and women cathect virtuosos. Both men and women associate musical virtuosity with sexual virtuosity, which tends to frighten men who don't see themselves as gay and fascinate men who do. Allan Keiler is one of the former, or so I'd like to think. Ken Russell, who directed *Lisztomania* (1975), is one of the latter—as am I.

Liszt himself appreciated this phenomenon and loved being loved by male audience members. In fact, he idealized them, as can be seen in his reading of a painting by Raphael. *Saint Cecilia*, according to Liszt, features figures who epitomize "the differential effects [music] has on the heart of man." Mary Magdalene "is captivated by the sensual appeal" of music but doesn't understand its "divine essence." Saint Paul hears music as a "form of eloquence" and means of "preaching [the] truth." Saint Augustine worries whether music contains hidden "poison." Saint John, however, "'the disciple whom Jesus loved,' the one to whom He entrusted His mother when dying, the one who by placing his head on the Master's breast learned the secrets of boundless . . . love," is the "perfect symbol" of affectionate audition—"tender and profound, yet strengthened by the salutary lessons of sorrow."[6] Unfortunately, most of the disciples Liszt idealized weren't quite as attuned to the homoerotic basis of their calling. When 21-year-old Karl Klindworth heard Liszt perform *Un Sospiro*, the étude Stefan plays a lot, he "was seized with a desire to study with him," but not, to his knowledge, with a desire to place his head upon the Master's breast (Walker, *Liszt* 2: 184).

Even though I applaud Liszt's appreciation, I don't endorse his discriminatory and misogynist attitude. In my book, Mary Magdalene is as good as Saint John. I don't condemn Lisa Berndle. Nor do I condemn Ophuls's Lola Montez, the inept ballerina Stefan is supposed to resemble. Lola may not be very good at ballet, an incapacity she, like Gide, attributes to poor "classical training." But she's good enough, and sexy enough, to attract an impressive array of lovers, a capacity I'd enjoy as well. ("Lola's" usually get what they want—think of *Damn Yankees*.) Or I would enjoy it if Lola-esque promiscuity, like Stefan's, yet for different reasons, didn't diminish one's cultural capital. Lola becomes a bad dancer because she's been a bad girl, not because she's missed a few lessons. Stefan becomes a bad pianist because he's been a bad *boy*, another story altogether.

Liszt, it should come as no surprise, is one of Lola's lovers. So is Chopin. But whereas Liszt is shown in the film, Chopin is simply mentioned in passing. Is Chopin's sexuality utterly unrepresentable? Not exactly. Chopin's sexuality, like Liszt's, is imaginable, but in a different register. It's imaginable in a movie like King Vidor's *A Song to Remember* (1945), in which we do see Chopin (Cornel Wilde) have a long affair with George Sand (Merle Oberon)—as well as have a close, and somewhat fictitious, friendship with Liszt. (Wilde—unlike Chopin, tall and muscular—was a star American audiences did find sexy.) As with *Lola Montès*, however, we don't see the two pianists sexualized all at once. Liszt has no love life whatsoever in *A Song to Remember*. Nor does he have much of a musical life. In fact, he plays only Chopin's music, including the *Funérailles* Polonaise, a piece we actually get to see him cathect. (In a remarkable scene set in the Pleyel headquarters, Liszt starts sight-reading the Polonaise, meets Chopin, and joins him in a duo piano version, Liszt playing the thunderous left-hand part, Chopin playing the non-thunderous right-hand.) Nor is Liszt the only one invested in the "manly" Polonaise. Friedrich Kalkbrenner, another piano virtuoso, loves the left-hand octaves as well. And once Chopin forsakes Jozef Elsner (Paul Muni), a manipulative bachelor who wants him to give big concerts and compose "serious" music, for Sand, a castrating bitch who wants him to compose salon music (the Nocturnes, the Berceuse, etc.) and *not* to concertize, he can't seem to finish writing it—much to the old man's chagrin.[7] Chopin, Elsner feels, is now a "fop." He even tells Chopin so, which prompts the composer to leave Sand, abandon the salon, finish the Polonaise, and perform it and other "serious" work in concert.[8] (Serious, for Hollywood, means loud and fast). Chopin, worn out, dies shortly thereafter, but we're not quite sure what killed him. Was it heterosexual castration or homosocial manipulation?

Both pianists do make love in James Lapine's *Impromptu* (1991). They also make their own music. But the lovemaking and music making are still dissimilar. Liszt (Julian Sands) makes vigorous love to Marie d'Agoult (Bernadette Peters), another castrating bitch. (Peters's part might have been written by Keiler's Walker.) Chopin (Hugh Grant), however, makes clumsy love to Sand (Judy Davis), who sees the Pole as a disembodied "angel" and treats him like a child. She even tells him "drink your milk," one of her better lines. (D'Agoult, who calls Chopin a "woman," takes things one step further.) The casting reinforces this differentiation. Sands is the actor who, in a moment of panic, refused the title role in *Maurice* (1987), a Merchant-Ivory production, and had to be replaced by James Wilby. Grant is the actor who played Clive, Maurice's aristocratic—and equally panicky—lover. Sands, moreover, sports his own Lisztean locks, whereas Grant, who happens to be prettier and to have nicer hair, wears an awful wig. (Grant's first line, "This summer dust is ruinous to my lungs," comes across as "This summer dust is ruinous to my looks"—a function of his foreign accent and disappointing appearance.) The scoring reinforces the differentiation as well. The first and only Liszt we hear is *Mazeppa*, a hypermasculine—and hypersex-ual—Transcendental Etude.[9] The first Chopin is the hyper-feminine E-flat major section of the first Ballade. He even skips the coda.

But even though we never hear the coda, even though *Mazeppa* is *Impromptu*'s only macho masterpiece, the scoring can also be said to undermine the differentiation. Liszt is a better pianist than Chopin, and Chopin knows it. (Chopin prefers Liszt's rendition of the "Aeolian Harp" Etude.)[10] Cho-pin, however, is a better composer, and everyone knows it. We know it. Sand knows it. D'Agoult knows it. Even Liszt knows it. (He blames d'Agoult, for having been a pretty miserable muse.) The film cites, but doesn't endorse, several conven-tional explanations for this, including the myth of Chopin's divine, as against Liszt's satanic, inspiration. (Sand may see Chopin as an "angel," but we don't.) The only explanation it does endorse concerns Chopin's virtual *un*conventionality, a peculiar—and (post)modern—characteristic Sand, a not-so-pretty proto-feminist muse, happens to foster. As in *A Song to Remember*, Grant's Chopin needs someone to help him fin-ish an important composition. But instead of needing Elsner to polish off his phallogocentric Polonaise, he needs Sand—a phallic mother who represents liberation, not castration—to put his "effortless" (and eponymous) Fantasie-Impromptu to bed. It's Sand who lets him release his creative—and pro-creative—juices. It's Sand, moreover, who has him embrace an improvisatory sexuality and an improvisatory musicality that seem both Gidean and Barthesian. Gidean, insofar as the liberty is illusory. (Chopin, unlike Schumann, is always in con-trol of texts that sound out of control.) Barthesian, insofar as it's utopian. *Impromptu* ends not with Chopin's death, but with the departure for Sand's Majorca, a fantasy island where anything passionate can happen.

Many of these ideologies are, of course, residual. The modern recognition of Chopin's musical mastery supersedes a Victorian devaluation,[11] but stems from Schumann's famous declaration, "Hats off, gentlemen, a genius!" (*Schumann on Music* 15). Liszt's technical mastery, which many of us take for granted, is a Romantic notion as well. Anyone can play Chopin and Liszt and decide for herself which one she prefers. But we can't hear *them* play. So if we really want to know which was the better virtuoso, or the more "sexual" virtuoso, we have to turn to contemporary accounts, many of which do, in fact, anticipate the differentiations the films represent, as well as differentiations pertaining to twentieth-century pianists.

Before we do so, however, please note two phenomena. The first is historical. Whereas nineteenth-century virtuosos made their own music, twentieth-century pianists interpret nineteenth-century music. Liszt, for example, performed a lot of Liszt. So did Horowitz, who also performed a lot of Schubert, Schumann, and Chopin. Consequently, sexual figurations of Liszt's playing are figurations of his (self-expressive) music as well. Sexual figurations of Horowitz, however, don't depend upon *what* he played. Rubinstein, after all, had the same repertoire. The second phenomenon is relatively transhistorical. Many celebrities are paired and polarized. Some such pairs, however, aren't polarized sexually. Think of Raphael and Michelangelo, Verdi and Wagner, Henry James and Edith Wharton, Joan Crawford and Bette Davis.[12] Consequently, the kinds of claims once made about Liszt and Chopin, Rubinstein and Horowitz, and others, as well as the kinds of claims I'm now making, aren't necessarily limited to musical performance artists. They are, however, limited to *sexualized* celebrities.

Romantic auditors did, in fact, polarize Liszt and Chopin. They also polarized Liszt and Thalberg. And in some respects, Chopin and Thalberg, as opposed to Liszt, were seen as interchangeable. Liszt was the more attractive, as well as the more visually dynamic. Chopin, according to Heinrich Heine, was "slender" and "frail" (Liszt, *Artist's Journey* 224). Liszt, according to Charles Hallé, was "remarkably beautiful" (Schonberg, *Great Pianists* 164). Chopin and Thalberg, like Clementi and Kalkbrenner, didn't gesticulate.[13] (Later such players include Tausig, Rachmaninov, and Horowitz.) Liszt, like Beethoven, did.[14] This combination of good looks and muscularity spelled sex appeal, the thing *American* audiences are supposed to appreciate. According to Heine, who coined the term Lisztomania, Liszt wasn't "placid":

When he sits down at the piano, sweeps his long hair back several times, and starts to improvise, he often hurls himself furiously at the ivory keys. . . . He overpowers and enflames you at one and the same time, but the feeling of being overpowered predominates. (Liszt, *Artist's Journey* 221)

According to Moritz Saphir, Liszt overpowered and enflamed the *piano*:

[Liszt] treats his mistress—the piano—now tenderly, now tyranically, devours her with kisses, lacerates her with lustful bites, embraces her, caresses her, sulks with her, scolds her, rebukes her, grabs her by the hair, clasps her then all the more delicately, more affectionately, more passionately, more flamingly, more meltingly; exults with her to the heavens, soars with her through the skies and finally settles down with her in a vale of flowers covered by a canopy of stars. (Loesser 369)

No one saw Chopin and Thalberg this way. Nor did anyone *hear* them this way. I'll delay the aural differentiations for a moment, because I can't ignore Saphir's presumption. Is the piano womanly? And, if so, which piano? The spinet? The concert grand? Unlike violins, violas, and cellos, pianos aren't exactly curvaceous. They don't resemble the female form. They do, however, connote femininity. Pianos connote the generations of women who've been forced to play—and teach—them. They also connote the women who played clavichords and harpsichords. But early-nineteenth-century concert grands, iron-framed and touch-sensitive precursors of modern instruments, were both masculine and feminine. They still connoted femininity, professional as well as amateur. (There were more female virtuosos in the nineteenth century than in the twentieth.) And they still enabled introverted lyricism—the *piano* component of the pianoforte. But they also enabled extroverted percussion—the *forte* component. They enabled, in other words, the brawny banging most of us associate with (Lisztian) virtuosity—and some of us associate with (Barthesian) amateurism.

The aural differentiations echo this instrumental androgyny. Chopin, a lyrical "poet," murmured. (Recall Thalberg's reaction to Chopin: "I need some noise, because I've heard nothing but pianissimo all evening.") Liszt, a "brilliant" orator, hammered. And Thalberg, notwithstanding the reaction, tended to be somewhat Chopinesque.[15] He favored wispy arpeggiation Liszt himself tried to emulate. *Un Sospiro* is one such attempt.

Cognoscenti did, in fact, en-gender the two sounds. Ignaz Moscheles, for example, found Chopin's music "too sweet, not manly enough, and hardly the work of a profound musician" (Schonberg, *Great Pianists* 124). They also conflated the visual and aural differentiations. Even Schumann, who knew a thing or two about split personalities, failed to keep his senses straight:[16]

Thalberg . . . was thought of as [Liszt's] competitor. But one had only to compare the two heads. I remember the observation of a well-known Viennese cartoonist who likened Thalberg's, not inaptly, to that of a beautiful countess with a man's nose. Of Liszt's head he said that any painter could use it as a model for a Greek god. Much the same could be said of their playing. (*Schumann on Music* 159)

Sight and sound, however, aren't the only couple to collapse under the strain of differentiation. All polar oppositions, including the gender—or sexual—differentiations assigned to Chopin, Liszt, and Thalberg, fall apart. Or come together. (I'm not suggesting Chopin's femininity "homosexualized" him. The notion's far too tidy and anachronistic. I am suggesting Chopin's femininity problematized what *we'd* call his sexuality.) Moscheles found Chopin unmanly at first inspection, but changed his mind when he heard the composer play: "Now . . . I understood his music. . . . The hard, inartistic modulations, so like those of a dilettante—which I can never manage when playing Chopin's music—cease to shock me" (Schonberg, *Great Pianists* 124). Schumann appropriated a likening of Thalberg to a countess, but a countess "with a man's nose." He also revealed a little secret, that Liszt was Chopinesque as well: "I would gladly sacrifice . . . the reckless bravura for the tender utterance, [and] excepting Chopin . . . know of none who could approach him in this kind of playing" (*Schumann on Music* 159).

A writer would call this collapse the law of the jungle. (After all, it is the law of *The Beast in the Jungle,* James's contribution to homosexual panic.)[17] A theorist would call it the logic of the supplement. A musicologist would call it the legacy of "expressive doubling."[18] Whatever the explanation, the thing to bear in mind is that the Romantic conflation of Liszt and Chopin, like the derivative one described in "Funérailles" ("my

father and brother are one person to me, as are Chopin and
Liszt"), went way beyond the occasional utterance. One legend has Chopin himself mistaking Liszt for Chopin upon hearing him play in a darkened room.[19] "You see," Liszt is supposed
to have said, "Liszt can be Chopin when he likes; but can Chopin be Liszt?" Well, yes, according to Fanny Mendelssohn, for
whom Chopin was the "perfect virtuoso" (Schonberg, *Great
Pianists* 146). (Fanny's standards, however, were Mendelssohn-
ian, and Felix was light-fingered.) And yes, according to *A
Song to Remember*, which, inverting the legend, has Chopin
mistaken for Liszt. The other thing to bear in mind is that the
Romantic conflation of Liszt and Thalberg went way beyond
the man's nose. It even went beyond the playful criticism of
Friedrich Wieck, Clara Schumann's father, who said that
whereas Liszt played with "inspired affectation," Thalberg
played with "inspired vacuity"—a distinction without a difference if ever there was one (Schonberg, *Great Pianists* 163).
It extended to the spin that settled the matter.

   Parisians had been spoiling for a Liszt-Thalberg showdown
long before Princess Cristina Belgiojoso, the spin-ster, arranged
for both men to perform in her salon. Hector Berlioz, having
heard his "Hammerklavier," championed Liszt: "Had [Bee-
thoven] himself returned from the grave, a paroxysm of joy . . .
would have swept over him." (There's that *Weihekuss* again.)
François-Joseph Fétis, however, championed Thalberg. The
pianists entered the fray as well: Thalberg refusing to give a
joint recital with the quip, "I do not like to be accompanied";
Liszt responding, "[Thalberg] is the only man I know who
plays the violin on the piano." (Walker, *Liszt* 1: 237) (I'm not
sure what Liszt meant and, given his emulation of Paganini,
find the comment rather ambiguous.) And the *Gazette musicale*, five days before the play-off, published the following ad-

vertisement: "The greatest interest . . . will be without question the simultaneous appearance of two talents whose rivalry at this time agitates the musical world, and is like the indecisive balance between Rome and Carthage. Messrs. Liszt and Thalberg will take turns at the piano" (March 26, 1837).

Thalberg, in fact, played first, offering the *Moses* Fantasy. Liszt followed with his own operatic paraphrase, the *Niobe* Fantasy. (I'll note, but won't dwell upon, the counterintuitive gendering: Moses is male, Niobe female.) The "revolutionary" princess then uttered the aphorism that became one of her claims to fame: "Thalberg is the first pianist in the world— Liszt is the only one" (La Mara, *Liszt und die Frauen* 42). The spin is senseless, of course—what difference does it make?— but no one seems to have noticed. According to one contemporary description:

Never was Liszt more controlled, more thoughtful, more energetic, more passionate; never has Thalberg played with greater verve and tenderness. Each of them prudently stayed within his harmonic domain, but each used every one of his resources. It was an admirable joust—the most profound silence fell over that noble arena. And finally Liszt and Thalberg were both claimed victors by this glittering and intelligent assembly. It is clear that such a contest could only take place in the presence of such an Areopagus. Thus two victors and no vanquished; it is fitting to say with the poet ET AD HUC JUDICE LIS EST. (Janin)

Nowadays, of course, Thalberg is relatively unknown—another reason the spin is senseless. No one plays his music. No one claims to be student of one of his students' students. History, in other words, has belied Belgiojoso's gracious judgment. In fact, it's belied her judgment in more ways than one. We still polarize and sexualize pianists. Even though we're less invested in turning pianists into pinups—the erotic attention

Liszt attracted is now paid to singers (Frank Sinatra, Elvis Presley, etc.), a fact of which Ken Russell, who cast rock star Roger Daltrey in *Lisztomania*, is well aware—we're more invested in celebrity secrets, sexual ones in particular. And we still depolarize, or conflate, pianists. But unlike Schumann, Wieck, and Belgiojoso, we don't do so somewhat deliberately. Since we are forced to distinguish between homosexuality and heterosexuality in ways and for reasons that rarely occured to Romantic counterparts, our conflations are, in fact, deconstructive—or to put it mildly, completely inadvertent.

We—we, that is, who don't "believe" in bisexuality—categorize modern pianists, like all men, as either gay or straight. They may not see themselves that way, make love that way, or *want* to make love that way. They may not play their own music. We, however, still find them self-expressive, associate self-expression with sexual orientation, and take full advantage of the homophobic stereotypes nineteenth-century predications of Chopin, Liszt, and Thalberg begin to suggest. In other words, we take advantage of most of the epithets Keiler hurls at Walker. And then some.

Why only "most" of Keiler's epithets? We do call gay pianism naive, superficial, pathological, and infantile. We don't call it unrealistic, gossipy, and misogynist. (Stereotypes may be sticky, but they don't stick everywhere.) Why "and then some"? We also call gay pianism neurotic, artificial, miniature, eccentric, incoherent, and self-indulgent.[20] Take Glenn Gould. For George Steiner, who finds Gould's love life "mysterious," the playing is "narcissistic." For Edward Said, who finds Gould's lips "decadent" and suggestive of "secret vice," the playing is "mannered," "immature," and "uncommitted" (22, 24, 30, 32). For Anton Kuerti, a pianist with "every reason to be insanely jealous" of Gould and whom Gould "ostracized" for hinting at "relationships [he] might have [had] with women," the playing is "shallow," "irresponsible," "perverse," "idiosyncratic," and reflective of the man's "moral turpitude."

Gould is exceptional, of course. He's the one twentieth-century virtuoso to avoid the concert stage, the Romantic repertoire, and the normal forms of social intercourse. Gould opens to nongay reading as well. Steiner, for example, celebrates the coherence, or "organic unity," of the self-indulgent playing (139). And while some critics analogize Gould's closeted style to that of Bobby Fischer,[21] another queer prodigy who valued his privacy, some analogize it to that of Liszt, a relatively nonqueer one. According to Will Crutchfield:

The comparison that keeps springing to mind is the great charismatic concert dropout of the last century, Franz Liszt. Accepting ours as an era in which the reproductive musician has partly displaced the composer as a defining figure, Gould is clearly the Liszt of his day: the combination of showmanship and high aspiration, the urge to display and the urge to withdraw, the extramusical interests, the reveling in technique and raw talent, and the sense that all this ought to be transcended and the haunting imperfection of the attempts to do so—no wonder Gould played scarcely a note of Liszt; it would have been too close for comfort. (25)

Lisztians also rely on the fact that both pianists moved around a lot. Crutchfield, for example, finds Gould's hyperactivity ("the big circles—the body swiveling from the pelvis, head and shoulders swaying wildly while the hands must hold their place") fascinating (25).

Nonetheless, the homophobic predication of Gould is typical—and archetypical. The predication is typical insofar as it's predominant, and archetypical insofar as Gould has become a touchstone of queer pianism. Ivo Pogorelich, for example, is known as "the Glenn Gould of the romantic piano"

(Schonberg, *Great Pianists* 460). (He's also known as the Brooke Shields of the Romantic piano [Mach 2: 248].) Horowitz, whose homosexuality remained an open secret even after the homosocial marriage to Wanda Toscanini,[22] is Gouldian as well. (Horowitz fell for the conductor, not the daughter.) Or so we say now that neither pianist is alive. Bernard Holland's self-deconstructive discussion of the matter is worth quoting at length:

> What troubles me is . . . the possibility that we are remembering Gould and Horowitz for the wrong reasons. In life, the two men were at opposite poles of music; in death they are startlingly alike. Here first were two eccentrics; Horowitz with a sweeping, electric, almost thoughtless iconoclasm that created some of the most exciting, and musically suspect, performances of the 20th century. Gould was a rebel with a cause; his carefully considered assaults on received knowledge had an electricity of their own.
>
> Both were immense talents. It was their musical accomplishments that got them to the threshold of celebrity, but it was something else that carried them over. Gould and Horowitz had the cachet to capture the attention of those who never heard them play: Horowitz with his weird touring life style and his intricate demands in matters of food and lodging; Gould, bundled against the cold in August, with his own adjustable piano stool and a stance at the piano that placed his nose roughly at the level of the keyboard. Their retreats from public life into silence were always accompanied by a curious amount of noise.
>
> Musically, Horowitz ignored style and rearranged accents, dynamics, phrase marks and tempos to suit his considerable, if Quixotic, musical imagination. Gould carved up style in carefully thought-out forays.

Holland would revive the polar opposition, but can't.[23] He cites one telling difference—Horowitz was thoughtless, Gould thoughtful—but more than one telling similarity. Both pianists, for Holland (against his better judgment), remain eccentric, unconventional, and reclusive. Does this make Holland homophobic? Consider his conclusion:

> The Gould-Horowitz iconography is an intoxicating one. It appeals to the youthful sap in all of us. It says that individuality liberates and that our parents knew meaningless things. Tradition is to be questioned—painstakingly, suspiciously—but music ignores tradition at its peril. Let Gould and Horowitz astonish you for the entrancing curiosities that they were. Then put them to the side of music, where they belong.

Put them to the side, where they belong. Punish them for having scorned the Law of the Father. Holland is grappling with the undeniable centrality of queer pianism—with the fact that even he recognizes the "immensity" of talent he'd like to marginalize. Well, why *do* people pay Pogorelich so much? So much more than, say, Andras Schiff? Why do we find Horowitz so electrifying? So much more electrifying than, say, Rubinstein? Talent alone can't account for this centrality. After all, Victorians marginalized Chopin despite his brilliance. Nor can the notion that most of us are "secretly" queer. Barthes may prefer Gould to Rubinstein for that reason, or may think he does,[24] but there's no (one) such thing as a queer "sensibility," secret or otherwise. One reason we do love queer pianists—if they're talented—is that we enjoy vicarious transgression. We love watching people break laws we are afraid to ignore. Another reason we love talented queer pianists is that we enjoy the spectacle of the closet. We love knowing more about gay men than they seem to know themselves. The more flamboyant, and the more ignorant, the better. Why else do we find Proust's Charlus so attractive?[25] Why else do we find the ostracism of Kuerti entertaining?[26] Why else do we relish the fact that Horowitz, who should have known better, had been married? Why else do we relish the fact that Pogorelich is married—to one of his piano teachers? On the other hand, "the more flamboyant the better" is somewhat hyperbolic. Liberace, unlike Wilde, seemed too queer to be taken seriously, a topic I'll turn to in my final chapter.

"Why do we find Horowitz more electrifying than, say, Rubinstein?" The comparison is, of course, no accident. Horowitz, who outflanked a number of competitors (Rudolf Serkin, Claudio Arrau, Artur Schnabel), and who, unlike Saphir's Liszt, used the piano to screw the *audience*,[27] is always compared to Rubinstein. "To the world," writes David Dubal, "Horowitz and Rubinstein were the masters of the grand manner, the Romantics par excellence." But where Rubinstein was "extroverted and healthy," Horowitz was "enigmatic and neurotic." Where Rubinstein "lived 'in the moment,'" Horowitz lived "for the piano—his very being and identity were linked to his instrument." Rubinstein understood musical structure and aroused an audience "to a high pitch of excitement." Horowitz focused on "pianistic detail" and gave an audience a "shock" it never forgot. Rubinstein found everything easy, saw life as funny, and "thought with his head." Horowitz found everything difficult, saw life as tragic, and "thought with his feelings" (*Evenings* 160, 161, 168). Schonberg reiterates Dubal's description. Rubinstein and Horowitz, he writes, "complemented one another." Rubinstein concerts were "comforting," Horowitz concerts "demonic." Rubinstein was "unmannered," "masculine," and "athletic." Horowitz was "mannered," "affected," "shallow," "neurotic," and "unfocused"—a pianist with an "affinity for miniatures" and a tendency to "become too engrossed in detail" (*Great Pianists* 434–60).

Are these homophobic predications, in Valley vernacular, for real? I'm afraid so. I have, of course, collated the predications in order to make fun of—and distance myself from—

them. The notion of Gould sounding "immoral" is especially ludicrous. So, too, is the notion of him sounding narcissistic. I've also found Horowitz's large-scale masterworks to be as coherent as those of his more Germanic competitors. The 1953 Schubert B-flat major Sonata, for example, is as good as if not better than Schnabel's—something many listeners, but few critics, could appreciate at the time.[28] The 1955 Clementi recording holds together as well. (Horowitz used to love his Clementi connection: he'd studied with Felix Blumenfeld, who studied with Anton Rubinstein, who studied with Alexander Villoing, who studied with John Field, who studied with Clementi.) People do, however, hear queer pianism homophobically. Even queer people. After all, it was well-meaning Virgil Thomson who first castigated Horowitz for his "affetuoso" style.[29] And queer pianists, like all queer people, do in fact (mis)recognize themselves homophobically, or stereotypically. Horowitz, for example, couldn't resist part of his predication. He admitted to playing simple music "artificially" (Schonberg, *Horowitz* 172–73) and hated his recording of Schumann's F minor Sonata. "It is so affected," he complained. "Why didn't somebody stop me? [The] playing is so neurotic. Schumann was crazy, but I ruined him" (Dubal, *Evenings* 206).

Affected, neurotic—what about infantile? How can a man with immense talent, the kind of talent that makes child prodigies seem older than they are, be characterized as babyish? Horowitz is seen as infantile, not because he played the C-sharp minor Prélude, but because he played the *enfant terrible*. (Rubinstein, of course, played the *grand seigneur*.)[30] He's also seen as infantile because, like Chopin ("drink your milk"), he's not supposed to handle large forms well. This conflation—of miniaturism and immaturity—has quite a pedigree, one that extends to Schumann. It was Schumann who, despite his recognition of Chopin's genius, failed to comprehend the B-flat minor, or "Funeral March," Sonata. "That he should have called it a 'sonata,'" he wrote, "suggests a joke, if not sheer bravado. He seems to have taken four of his most unruly children and put them together, possibly thinking to smuggle them, as a sonata, into company where they might not be considered individually presentable." (*Schumann on Music* 173) Talk about the pot calling the kettle black! If you haven't heard them very often and so wouldn't have an amateurish notion of their structure, just try to make conventional sense of the Schumann Sonatas, Op. 11 (F-sharp minor) in particular. Yet for all the critics who reiterate this complaint, as well as this configuration,[31] few do so in relation to Schumann. And few do so in relation to Liszt, who's equally problematic and whose B minor Sonata is no more coherent than Chopin's.[32] Many critics, however, do so in relation to Horowitz, who happened to have integrated the Liszt Sonata and who, to his credit, resisted the Schumannesque predication.[33] Horowitz may have been affected and neurotic, but he never *belittled* himself.

The opposition of Horowitz and Rubinstein, unlike the opposition of Chopin and Liszt, doesn't deconstruct itself. Liszt may have been the better pianist, but Chopin was the better musician—and so, sexually speaking, they both come out on top. It is Rubinstein, however, who is seen as the better musician, and Horowitz the better pianist—and so Rubinstein alone, but for his rival's greater (and thoroughly declassé) popularity, comes out on top. (Another reason we devalue virtuosity, according to Said, is that we associate it with "dangerous effeminacy" [62]—think of Horowitz as the Queen of the Night.) Even Rubinstein thought so, notwithstanding—or perhaps due to—the fact that he envied Horowitz's technical mastery. Retrospectively and stereotypically he writes:

Deep within myself, I felt I was the better musician. My conception of the sense of music was more mature, but at the same time, I was conscious of my terrible defects—of my negligence for detail, my treatment of some concerts as a pleasant pastime, all due to that devilish facility for grasping and learning the pieces and then playing them light-heartedly in public; with all the conviction of my own musical superiority, I had to concede that Volodya was by far the better pianist (256).

No, the Horowitz/Rubinstein opposition needs something, or someone, else to come undone. Just as the opposition homo/hetero needs bisexuality, and bisexuals, Horowitz/Rubinstein needs what Barthes would call a "third term." And it has one. We call it, we call him, Van Cliburn.

Cliburn is the queer pianist who plays it straight. He looks stereotypically gay—a bachelor who worshiped the mother (Rildia Bee) he studied under and lived with—but doesn't sound it. His "golden" tone and structural savvy remind people of Rubinstein and not of Horowitz, even though they overworked the same warhorses and even though they both retired early. (Horowitz retired for reasons having to do with "nervous" exhaustion, Cliburn for ones having to do with a sense that "his playing got limper and limper" [Horowitz 491]). Take Tchaikovsky's first Piano Concerto.[34] According to *Joseph* Horowitz, who could be a lot nicer to his namesake:

Horowitz made the concerto a fractured vehicle—it barely holds together—for convulsive athletic prowess. Cliburn makes the concerto more than a vehicle. [He] conceives the work as a testament to romantic yearning and loss. In Horowitz's reading, the most telling moment is the octave volcano signaling the last, distended reprise of the finale's big tune. (264)

Or take Rachmaninov's third (*Rocky III*, in Juilliard parlance). Joseph writes:

Horowitz conveys—exaggerates—Rachmaninoff's nervous instability. But the interpretation as a whole, with its superabundant surface detail, is emotionally unfocused. Cliburn's fingers never brag. His tone is not kaleidoscopically varied but invariably round, burnished, unforced. The long lines he intuits sing beautifully of sadness and nostalgia. His course is steady and farsighted. Its current heaves upward in great concentrated waves, slowing the pace, weighting the climaxes. The first-movement cadenza, the concerto's central storm point, an upheaval of expanding force and sonority, builds with utter sureness; Cliburn simply lets it come. The tidal altitude and breadth of its crest are dizzying. The long descent is equally thorough; to begin the coda, the first theme returns dazed and spent. (30)

The orgasmic imagery seems overblown, of course, but if you listen to Cliburn's recording, you'll realize Joseph is justified. Dazed and spent, you too will come to think of Horowitz and Rubinstein, and—with a tinge of *tristesse*, or perhaps a sense of relief—feel compelled to reconsider their sexual relation. You'll say to yourself, If a mama's boy like Cliburn can play like *that*, maybe he's not really queer. And you'll even say to yourself, Maybe the Horowitz octaves, the famous "athletic" octaves, *weren't* very "convulsive." After all, they sound perfectly fine—or, in other words, Rubinsteinian—in the Schubert.

We can now begin to appreciate the castration of Stefan Brand. Stefan is read as effeminate, and even a bit gay, because he's the kind of pianist who reminds people of Chopin and Horowitz, not of Liszt and Rubinstein, and because he predates Cliburn. He may play *Un Sospiro*, but he plays it the way he looks—and he looks like a dandy. There's another reason as well, one I've mentioned in passing. Even though we correlate musical and sexual virtuosity, we sense that sexual expenditure reduces cultural capital. Freud, of course, popularized this notion—call it masculine "sublimation"—but it's been around for quite some time. The Romantics, for example, had a version of it, as did the Victorians. So the version we know and experience—I, for example, haven't had sex with anyone since I began this book—should be seen as neo-Romantic and neo-Victorian as well as postmodern.

The Victorian version of "sublimation" was, in fact, somewhat Romantic. Men could belong to a "seminal economy" long before Victorian sexologists made sure everyone did. Romantic artists who womanized and Romantic boys who masturbated might jeopardize their potential creativity and procreativity simply by ejaculating. (For some reason, we don't really "count" masturbation anymore. Nor do we police it.) To quote Balzac, "There goes another novel [*Encore un roman foutu*]." The Romantic ideology, however, was merely emergent. It hadn't yet come to dominate Western culture, which is why Byron was a bit of a Don Juan and why Liszt's Byronic sex life didn't cost him anything. In other words, no stories circulate about Liszt's having said, "There goes another concert étude." Liszt, however, lived a lot longer than Byron. Ten years into Victoria's reign, he retired from concertizing in order to devote himself to the music of Weimar. And 25 years into her reign, he retired from the womanizing that concertizing facilitated in order to devote himself to composition— the ultimate (Chopinesque) musicianship—and to God. He had to, in fact. No one would have credited the last creations, or the final calling, if he'd kept it up.

We still think along these lines. Many of us prefer the serious music Liszt wrote when celibate to the pyrotechnical music he wrote when dissolute. And the few of us who don't know what we're up against—economics, psychoanalysis, and elitist (or envious) devaluation of musical virtuosity. To quote Charles Rosen, a serious musician with technique to burn:

I've always thought him a very great composer, but I have, I must say, very odd taste in Liszt. The fashion nowadays is to like the very late pieces, the strange experimental pieces. But I prefer the early pieces. I think that old war-horse the First Concerto is an absolute masterpiece. I also think the *Paganini Etudes* are very great. . . . And the great Fantasy on Themes from *Don Giovanni* is extraordinary. (Dubal, *Reflections* 275)

Most of us, moreover, prefer to imagine the virtuosos we can't ignore (the spectacular ones, the "musical" ones) as either virginal or uxorious. We publicize the continence of the unmarried ones (Gould, Cliburn) and the fidelity of the married ones (Horowitz, Rubinstein). Or we have them publicize it for us. We know an awful lot about Wanda, for example, including the notion that she kept Horowitz on a tight leash. (No whips, though—no cock rings either.) And we know a lot about Aniela (Mlynarska), including the notion that Rubinstein didn't play very well until he settled down and raised a family. (Saved!—as Stefan might have been.)

On the other hand, we also know that Rubinstein didn't "submit to disciplined practicing" until he'd heard Horowitz (Dubal, *Evenings* 161). Which is the case? Both, and neither. Rubinstein himself believed the two accounts. He even suggests he married "Nela" out of pianist envy—or, in other words, homosocially:

My thoughts were constantly occupied with Nela and the problem of marriage. My self-esteem was at its lowest. The pianistic exuberance and the technical ease of Vladimir Horowitz made me feel deeply ashamed of my persistent negligence and laziness in bringing to life all the possibilities of my natural musical gifts. I knew that I had it in me to give a better account of the many works which I played in concerts with so much love and yet with so much tolerance for my own lack of respect and care. It came to a point where I seriously considered giving up my ambition of a great pianistic career to become a piano teacher. (258)

Well, I don't buy it. (Surprised? You should be.) To tell the truth (*my* truth), to demystify the ideology (*our* ideology), Rubinstein's pre-Horowitz recordings are quite as dazzling as his post-Horowitz. Either Rubinstein had always "buckled down,"[35] and so didn't have a "natural" technique, or he never buckled down, and so did.

It's sad, really. We needn't rely upon the salvific, and far too commonplace, representation of the Rubinstein marriage. We needn't have men like Horowitz marry women like Wanda—or women like Wanda marry men like Horowitz. We needn't link men like Gould to the stereotypical sterility of the maiden piano teacher. Let Horowitz, Gould, and Cliburn out. Out of the closet, if that's where they are. And out into the "real" world I still imagine. The one where people perform sexually as well as professionally. The one where pianists make love as well as music. In other words, let them be Liszt—*early* Liszt.

One last anecdote. My friend Ron was in a West Village bar about fifteen years ago when an elderly Russian asked him, "What's your sign?" It was Horowitz, of course, and Ron was flustered. I'm not sure what I'd have said at the time, but if Horowitz were alive today and up to the same old trick, I'd probably respond, "Aquarius, or Ganymede—same as Clementi." And if all went well, we'd go to his place, where I'd dim the lights, have him play the Barcarolle, or maybe *Un Sospiro*, and let him ravish me.

Intermezzo

∿ Diana Graa, the teacher Dr. Train demonized, is a widow. Kathrine Parker, the teacher I shared with David Nish, is a spinster. Arlene Portney, the teacher—and friend—through whom I trace my Lisztean lineage (Portney studied with Sascha Gorodnitski, who studied with Alexander Siloti, who studied with Liszt), is a wife and mother, but was a "maiden" when I studied with her. I hate these mind-warping and male-oriented stereotypes. They misconstrue women, and make women misconstrue themselves. Why, then, do I use them?

CHAPTER 5

∿ *Music Lessons*

I know noble accents
And lucid, inescapable rhythms;
But I know, too,
That the blackbird is involved
In what I know.

Wallace Stevens, "Thirteen Ways
of Looking at a Blackbird"

∿ There aren't many women in this book, and most of the
ones I do include are teachers. Well, why *don't* I write about
female amateurs? Why, for example, do I trivialize Carol
Turchin? And why don't I write about female virtuosos?
(Koestenbaum does, more or less. He plays "like someone who
studied with someone who studied with Myra Hess" ["Piano
Life" l. 142].) Why, for example, don't I write about Martha
Argerich, who's sexier than Horowitz and whose Tchaikovsky
Concerto is the best on record?

Yes, I'm phallocentric. I prefer men—in bed. And yes, I'm
phallogocentric. I prefer to argue—in print. But does that
make me misogynistic? Do I dislike women just because I dislike *écriture feminine*—or bad *écriture feminine*? After all, many

of my favorite colleagues write like Mary Daly, something I'll
attempt as well. Do I dislike women just because—or despite
the fact that—I dislike feminine stereotypes, and in particular the stereotype "maiden piano teacher"? I don't *think* so.
After all, "some of my best friends," including my former
teacher Arlene Portney, are women. On the other hand, I'm
not very fond of Kathrine Parker.

I know I *should* be fond of her. In fact, I'd *love* to be fond
of her. But how can I learn to appreciate this problematic Other
—Parker in particular, the "maiden piano teacher" in general?
What's my methodology? I can't exactly remember her as
"nice" and at any rate am too cynical to be seduced by niceness. (*Niceness*, it's so—high school.) I can't look her up and
have her speak "for herself." She wouldn't know what to say
or, more to the point, what I need to hear. (Even I don't know
what I need—yet.) My methodology, as usual, is one *Parker*
taught me. I'll try to understand her by acting like a typical
student—and typical teacher, and typical writer. I'll *perform*
comprehension, and try to please and impress the teacher—
the student, the reader. Only now that I teach cultural studies (now that I'm no longer learning concert etudes), I'll do
so by using the tools, the critical techniques, of my latest trade.
Why use them? Because the techniques do access Others who
can't, or whom we can't have, express themselves. How will I
use them? Nonparodically. Parody, here, would signal disbe-
lief I'd rather suspend and insecurity I'd rather transcend.
(The insecurity: that I haven't really mastered techniques I'm
willing to take seriously.) And unscientifically. I'm Barthesian,
not Althusserian. I approach the Other from *within* our mythic
relationship and intersubjectivity. After all, she's "involved in
what I [want to] know." And I myself am now a maiden piano teacher—a supposed celibate who proffers critical, as op-

posed to musical, capital to bourgeois kids who, by and large, aren't very interested in it. And so, "Thirteen Ways of Looking at a Maiden Piano Teacher." A fragmentary *tour de force*? A miniature fiasco?[1]

Lyrical

Wayne Koestenbaum begins "Piano Life" with a work Horowitz mastered and an equivocation I find suggestive:

> Today I sightread the last
> Schubert sonata: he wanders between keys: evasive
>
> and elementary, his melodies
> meander. Tipsy Schubert,
>
> if I were to return to 1974 for a piano lesson,
> would my teacher say, "You've ruined your life,"
>
> or would she just say "hello,"
> and with her faraway "hello"
>
> would possibilities cluster around my feet like clouds
>   above the Andes?
>
>   (ll. 1–9)

I, too, would lyricize the maiden piano teacher. (Contrary to popular belief, poetry can be critical. So can camp.) I, too, would provide oblique answers to nostalgic questions.

If *I* were to return to 1974 for a piano lesson, would Miss Parker say, "You've ruined your life," or would she just say "hello"? She'd *never* say, "You've ruined your life." She'd probably say, "You've *saved* your life—by not becoming a concert pianist (you don't have what it takes), by not becoming a piano teacher (you wouldn't like it), and by being an amateur (nothing wrong with that)." Why, then, the intimation of disgrace? Why did these women terrorize us? Because their teachers terrorized them? (Kathrine Parker as Rosina Lhevinne:

"VOT IS ALL DIS BANGING!!?"—only without the Russian accent.) Because their mothers did? Their fathers? Terror, in fact,
isn't a very efficient learning device. (Children need cheer-
leaders, not drill sergeants.) And teachers shouldn't act like
parents, or like abusive parents, even though it can be hard
not to. Especially when you care for the kid.

She'd just say, "hello," and with that "hello" possibilities
would cluster like clouds above the Andes. The possibility that
other adults (adults not paid to) will have found me special
and have tried to cultivate me. (The piano teacher is the primal mentor.) The possibility that I will have learned to do the
impossible—play Chopin, play Liszt. The possibility that I will
have found pleasure in the passé. (Regressive pleasure? Transgressive?) But the hello would be so "faraway." Why? Because
she'd rather be somewhere else? Or someone else? Or *with*
someone else? And if so, once again, why?

Campy

Jeffrey Swann's been on the rag since 1977, when she dropped
her fire baton and lost the Miss Universe pageant. Came in
third, to be precise—after Steven De Groote (of South Africa)
and Alexander Toradze (of the former Soviet Union). First
there were the tacky comments about Lili Kraus, who judged
the competition. Then there were the rumors about Youri
Egorov, who didn't even make the finals.[2] Now she's letting
Diana Graa have it: "[Young American pianists are] dominated by older women, many of whom have unfulfilled relationships with their [husbands and] encourage an undirected
sexuality. This may be one reason . . . there are an awful lot of
homosexual pianists" (Horowitz 137n).

Nurse, give Miss Swann some Pamprin. And while you're
at it, give some to Miss Horowitz (Miss *Joseph* Horowitz), who
calls this a "provocative" analysis of pianistic "pathology" and

an "illustrative" look at pedagogical "castration." *Unfulfilled* relationships? An *awful* lot of homosexual pianists? How would *they* know how much sex these women are having? (Maybe they do find their husbands fulfilling. Maybe they have affairs. Maybe they masturbate.) How would they know whether these women "castrate" us? (Maybe we're just born this way.) Or whether they *want* to castrate us. (Maybe they have other things on their mind, consciously or not.) And even if they do castrate us, why *blame* them? I, for one, enjoy being a girl. (I'm simply *fabulous*, Mrs. Graa. Thank you *so* much.) Anyway, you'd think a pianist who finds heterosexuality and homosexuality equally undesirable ("unfulfilled" and "awful") would rather be "undirected"—whatever that may mean.

Sentimental

Diana, it's me. Albert. I hear you're not doing too well. You're teaching again, but don't have many students. (Well, you *are* a little scary.) You're socializing again, but don't have many friends. (You never did, but you had *me*.) And that Kopelson kid is ruining your reputation. I wish he could see you through my eyes. He'd see a beautiful young woman who could have had anyone, but married an elderly invalid, and a gifted pianist who could have concertized, but taught in order to support him. I do love you, Diana. I love your playing, your kindness, your devotion, your generosity. I even love you enough to wish you'd remarried, because you'd have been so much happier. More money, more room, more comfort. More company. (Really, Diana, all those cats!) Or has the memory of our marriage sufficed? It has for me. I've been thinking of you, for the most part, and barely recall the life I led before we met. (Do you remember the beach? The cast-off kitten you made me take home?) I've been waiting for you, too.

What was the name of that piece you used to play? It's quite slow. It's in minor. I think it's by Scriabin. I hear it whenever I think of you, and am filled with sadness and longing.

Tropological

Metaphor: conceptual displacement. Metonymy: conceptual contiguity. Synecdoche: conceptual partiality. Knowledge, we know, is fundamentally figurative and therefore problematic.

The *metaphor* of the maiden piano teacher. Felisberto Hernández (1902–64) opens "The Stray Horse," one of his *Piano Stories*, with a description of Celina's studio:

First you saw only white: the large slipcovers on the piano and the sofa and the smaller ones on the chairs and armchairs. And underneath was the furniture, which you knew was black because of the legs sticking out from under the white skirts.

Once when I was alone in the room, I raised a chair's skirt and found that although the wood was black the seat was a silky green. (5)

Celina, it turns out, is the teacher the narrator had when he was ten, and a woman who bears a striking resemblance to her furniture:

Once when my hands were reaching out for the skirt of a chair they were stopped short by the loud noise of the hallway door as Celina hurried in from the street. I barely had time to pull the hands back when she came up in her usual way and kissed me. (The habit was ruthlessly suppressed as we parted one afternoon and she told my mother something in the order of, "This young gentleman is growing up and from now on we'll have to shake hands.") She was in black, her tall, slim figure bound tight in her heavy wool dress, as if she had run her hands many times down the curves formed by the corset to smooth out every wrinkle and then up to choke her neck in the high collar that reached to her ears. Topping it all was her very white face with very black eyes, a very white forehead and very black hair done up in a bun like that of a queen I had seen on some coins: it reminded me of a burned pudding.

I was just beginning to digest the surprise of Celina's noisy entrance and her kiss when she reappeared in the room. But now, over the stern black dress, she wore white: a starched smock of lightweight material that had short flared sleeves with ruffles. (10–11)

Presumably, Celina's seat is "silky green" as well. But what's a woman's "seat"? Her lap? Her soul? And what would it mean for it to be silky green?

The *metonymy* of the maiden piano teacher. We hear Celina play, and expect triumphant self-expression. We're disappointed.

My mother or my grandmother has asked her to play and she sits down at the piano. My grandmother must be thinking, "The teacher is going to play"; my mother: "Celina is going to play"; and I "*She* is going to play." . . . Celina says she is not sure she remembers the piece. She is nervous, and on her way to the piano she trips over a chair, which must make a noise—but we are not supposed to notice. She has gathered enough speed that the impulse carries her past the chair and the accident is immediately forgotten. She sits down at the piano: we are hoping nothing unpleasant happens to her. Before she begins, we have just enough time to imagine she will play something impressive which will make us recommend her to our acquaintances. She is so nervous, and so aware of being the teacher, that my grandmother and my mother both try to advance her a bit of success, willing their favorable expectations on her and anxiously awaiting the performance that will allow them to match their expectations with reality. . . .

When Celina performed for us that time I took in everything that reached my eyes and ears. Before that, I had been letting things become too familiar, until they had almost stopped surprising me and I no longer really appreciated what she did.

My mother and grandmother seemed to be halfway into a sigh from which they hung suspended, as if afraid that at the supreme moment, just when their effort to understand was supposed to take off, their wings would carry them about as far as useless hens' wings.

I was probably very bored, after a while. (26–28)

The *synecdoche* of the maiden piano teacher. We now know how little we know about Celina.

When the child's eyes seize a part of something, they think it is the whole thing. (And the child cares no more than a dream does whether his images are complete or similar to those of real life: he simply proceeds as if they were.) When the child looked at Celina's bare arm he felt the whole of her was in that arm. The eyes I have now want to capture Celina's mouth, but they can't define the shape of her lips in relation to the rest of her face; they want to grasp a single feature and are left with none. The parts have lost their mysterious relationship to each other, they have lost their balance and natural proportion and seem disconnected, as if a clumsy hand had drawn them. If the hand tries to get the lips to articulate a word, their movements are as forced as those of a wind-up doll. (29–30)

Narratological

What if Celina had been silent and hadn't played at all? This is a question to which we know the gnomic answer: "Those who can, do; those who can't, teach." [*Gnomic*: aphoristic; "made in a collective and anonymous voice originating in traditional human experience" (Barthes, *S/Z* 18).]

Louise Bogan (1897–1970) invokes this answer in writing autobiographically of a teacher she used to love.

Miss Cooper lived in my mind at a continual point of perfection; she was like a picture: she existed, but not in any degree did she live or change. She existed beyond simple human needs, beyond hunger and thirst, beyond loneliness, weariness, below the heights of joy and despair. (Limmer 41–42)

The crystallization ends, however, when, having questioned Miss Cooper's competence (the woman never demonstrates the skill she's paid to impart), Bogan sees her for what she is. [*Crystallization*: the process by which lovers succumb to "patterns of exquisite illusion" (Stendhal 128).]

One afternoon she came out of the kitchen and stood behind me. She had something in her hand that crackled like paper, and when she spoke she mumbled as if her mouth were full. I turned and looked at her; she was standing with a greasy paper bag in one hand and a half-eaten doughnut in the other. Her hair was still beautifully arranged; she still wore the silver and fire-opal ring on the little finger of her right hand. But in that moment she and the room died for me. She . . . had betrayed me. She . . . had let me down; she had appeared as she was: a tired old woman who fed herself for comfort. (42)

Who is speaking here? No one in particular, of course. But Bogan as well. Bogan in particular. Bogan, who *discredits* the gnomic answer:

A tired old woman who fed herself for comfort. With perfect ruthlessness I rejected her utterly. And for weeks, at night, in the bedroom of the frame house in Harold Street, I shed tears that rose from anger as much as disappointment, from disillusion and from dismay. I can't remember that for one moment I entertained pity for her. It was for myself that I kept that tender and cleansing emotion. Yes, it was for myself and for dignity and gentility soiled and broken that I shed those tears. At fifteen and for a long time thereafter, it is a monstrous thing, the heart. (42–43)

Pity? It's a pity autobiography isn't dialogical. Bogan does interrogate the gnomic answer, but she can't impersonate another position. She can't, for example, impersonate Miss Cooper, who may have antignomic, or paradoxical, questions of her own. Questions like: Need love be illusory? ("Couldn't you love me as I am? Couldn't you love me as a friend?") Need teachers be masterful? ("There is an age at which we teach what we know. Then comes an age at which we teach what we do not know. [Now] comes the age of unlearning, of yielding to the foreseeable change which forgetting imposes on the [knowledge] we have traversed" [Barthes, "Inaugural Lecture" 478].) And is pity all that tender and cleansing? ("Don't cry for me, Louise. I'm a doughty old woman who happens to like doughnuts, not a tired old woman who feeds herself for comfort.")

Mariological

The maiden teacher is a virgin mother. The maiden teacher of a child prodigy, *theotokos*. The maiden teacher of a child prodigy who forsakes her, *mater dolorosa*.

Madame Sousatzka (Shirley MacLaine) nurtures Manek Sen (Navin Chowdry), a brilliant fifteen-year-old, and can't let him go.[3] It's a pattern. Madame Sousatzka mothers all her gifted boys (abusively, as did her own mother). In fact, she infantilizes them. They "stay babies," even though she'd have them "become men." And she grieves when they finally leave the nest. "Of course I was in love with you," she tells one tearfully. "Isn't every mother in love with the son she creates?" Why do they leave? She's not *that* bad—just a *little* abusive. ("You're a failure," she yells at Manek, but only when he has one foot out the door.) She's not that bizarre—just a little batty. They leave Madame Sousatzka (her mother's maiden name) for other men. They leave her for the all-male world of the virtuoso. For male mentors and cohorts. (God the Father, John the Baptist, the apostles.) They also leave her for other women. Manek loses his virginity to maudlin Jenny (Twiggy) [Mary Magdalene] the night he decides to study with Leo Milev.

Is it worth it? Is raising children who go on to greater glory worth the trouble? Mary joins Jesus in heaven. Madame Sou-

satzka stays where she is: munching cookies ("Maman's rec-
ipe") in a seedy apartment, bullying boys who'll break her
heart, sneaking into concerts given by former students, en-
joying the vicarious thrill of hearing them play well in public
(but is it really enjoyable, or so very thrilling?), and knowing
they're *somewhat* grateful.

Mary-Daly-ological

Who is Madame Sousatzka? Beldame Sousatzka is a Virgin
who revels in be-ing Alone, a Virago who avoids the Coma-
tose State of matrimony. She's an Unsubdued Survivor, a Spin-
ster who twirls the thread of Life on her own axis and lives beyond the pale of patriarchy.

Is she ever sad? Not at all. Beldame Sousatzka is a Howling
Hag who frightens fools. She's a Raving Lunatic who laughs
out loud, and in laughing shatters the hierarchs' house of mirrors, defusing their power of deluding Others.

So she is *batty.* Yes, but batty in the way Bette Davis was
batty—Self-directed, Uncanny, Eccentric.

Who, then, is Manek Sen? Manek Sen is a fool. He's a phallic fool who resists Beldame Sousatzka's Archimagical charms
(*Arch-Image*: Mary: vestige of the Goddess symbol preserved
in christianity as a hook for Heathen masses; tamed Goddess
symbol intended to conceal the Background Memory of the
Arch-Image, but that functions to evoke Archaic Active Po-
tency in women). He's a wantwit who'd rather join a gynoci-
dal cockocracy (yahweh & son, steinway & sons) than belong
to a bevy of Wild Women (Gertrude Stein & Daughters) and
who'd rather conceive of The Incarnation (sublimated sexual
fantasy promulgated as sublime christian dogma; mythic su-
per-rape of the Virgin Mother) than comprehend an a-maz-
ing musical dis-covery.[4]

Psychoanalytic

Isabelle Vengerova (1877–1955), the piano teacher who, according to Curtis Institute lore, inspired the film *Madame Sousatzka*, was both abusive and idealistic. One student, Harry Neal, reports that lessons would begin with helpful instruction ("Let not the tiniest flaw slip from underneath your fingers" [94]) and end with hurtful interrogation ("Are you lazy or conceited—or just stupid?" [93]). Other students predicate her in similar terms:

"Autocratic, didactic, unsympathetic, impatient, destructive" . . . "A perfectionist, a terrible taskmaster (who expected more from her students than they were capable of)" . . . "Sincere, strict, a perfectionist" . . . "Intolerant (yet, underneath it all, warmhearted and compassionate)" . . . "Very thorough, very demanding" . . . "Strong-willed, authoritative (sometimes to the point of 'destroying' a student)" . . . "Profound, stoic, majestic, indomitable" . . . "Inspiring, unreasonable, dogmatic, dynamic" . . . "Tyrannical, relentless, awesome, authoritarian, uncompromising, overpowering" . . . "Inflexible, impersonal" . . . "Ominous, hypersensitive, erratic, 'Russian-paranoid,' devoted, loving, strong" . . . "Blunt, undiplomatic, impolite (but capable of curing pianistic diseases with a high degree of skill)" . . . "Dedicated, imperious, intransigent, demanding, totally devoid of personal vanity, a true idealist" . . . "Intimidating, egotistical, sadistic, cold and cruel" . . . "Overperfectionist." (Rezits 21–22)

Many Vengerova students—Leonard Bernstein, Gary Graffman, Gilbert Kalish, Jacob Lateiner—seem to have risen, or to want to rise, to the challenge. (Neal, "long after her death, [is] still trying to win [his] way back into her favor" [90].) Others do seem to have been "destroyed." (Vengerova, who could be "withering," tied little Betty Benthin up in "knots" [Rezits 22].)

But *why* did Vengerova involve them "in an unending search for perfection" and refuse to "let them settle into . . . mediocrity" (Neal 75, 86)? Why did she have to ruin—and then renovate—their self-esteem? ("What do you want of me? That I should pamper your little ego? No! For you my studio is a jungle, and in it you must fight for your life. Stand up like a man and I'll goad you, and I'll drive you, and I'll torment you until you grow into more than you know!" [Neal 101].) Because the ego ideal Vengerova introjected doesn't appear to have been impossible. She was a Theodor Leschetizky protégé who measured up to, and probably surpassed, his exacting standards. She *knew* she was a great teacher, moreover, and didn't credit the conventional wisdom that figures pedagogues as would-be performers. She had no desire to be Rudolf Serkin (the head of the Curtis piano department), even though she never played in public and so might have seen herself as a "failed concert artist," and even though she was a woman and so might have seen herself as a "failed man"—nearly irresistable constructions that happen to reinforce one another. Hence her "strength."

We can all learn from Madame Vengerova. Barthes, for example, would have been a lot happier had he wanted to be literary critic Raymond Picard, and not André Gide or Marcel Proust. Then again, we'd never know the pleasure of this self-critical writer's "writerly" criticism.

Semiotic

Nicolas Slonimsky studied with Vengerova—who was, as it happens, his aunt—soon after she left Leschetizky. She wasn't yet a perfectionist—not with a young relative, at any rate.

[My first concert] went off well. I tried to forget the few wrong notes I played, and my aunt did not mention these mistakes. She . . . was pleased with my "expression." (Slonimsky 3)

Barthes, too, studied with a maiden aunt—Aunt Alice, the only piano teacher he ever had and a woman even less demanding than Slominsky's Aunt Isabelle. Or so we gather from Barthes's own attitude toward the instrument:

If I play badly—aside from the lack of velocity, which is a purely muscular problem—it is because I fail to abide by the written fingering: I improvise, each time I play, the position of my fingers, and therefore I can never play anything without making mistakes. The reason for this is obviously that I want an immediate pleasure and reject the tedium of training, for training hampers pleasure—for the sake of a greater ulterior pleasure, as they say (we tell the pianist what the gods said to Orpheus: Don't turn back *prematurely* on the effects of your action). So that the piece, in the perfection attributed to it but never really attained, functions as a bit of a hallucination: I gladly give myself up to the watchword of a fantasy: "*Immediately!* " even at the cost of a considerable loss of reality. (*Roland Barthes* 70)

Like Barthes, Aunt Alice knows there's no such thing as a transcendental signifier. No rehearsal is flawless. No performance is perfect. So why listen to, or degrade, yourself? Simply *imagine* yourself playing better than you do. And like Isabelle, but for an unrelated reason, Alice was a happy pianist. Thanks to her proto-deconstructive insight, she didn't measure herself against an impossible musical standard and never tried to satisfy an unrealistic musical demand.

The insight Alice shared with her nephew is *pseudo*deconstructive as well. Even though they don't believe in transcendental signifiers, they do believe in transcendental *signifieds*. They believe in make-believe perfection, in hallucinatory virtuosity. If only Barthes had fantasized having *written* wonderfully. ("Listen to this, Aunt Alice. Don't I sound like Racine?")

Materialist

Miss Eckhart, the impoverished piano teacher in Eudora Welty's "June Recital," keeps her metronome locked in a safe.

It's the only thing she keeps in there, and she keeps it there long after she's lost her last student. Miss Eckhart sees the metronome as her pedogogic essence. ("The old woman held her possession [and] stood looking at the three people fixedly, as if she showed them her insides, her live heart" [85].) Jinny, a selfish student, sees it as a worthless fetish. Cassie, a devoted one, sees it as a bit of both:

> Miss Eckhart worshiped her metronome. She kept it, like the most precious secret in the teaching of music, in a wall safe. Jinny Love Stark, who was only seven or eight years old but had her tongue, did suggest that this was the only thing Miss Eckhart owned of the correct size to lock up there. . . .
>
> Cassie, out of nice feeling, looked the other way when it was time for the . . . opening of the safe. It seemed awful, and yet imminent, that . . . she, Cassie Morrison, might be the one to call logical attention to the absurdity of a safe in which there were no jewels, in which there was the very opposite of a jewel. (45–46)

However, male characters—Cassie's brother Loch, Old Man Moody, and Mr. Fatty Bowles—see it a bit differently. They see the metronome as a bomb.

If only it were. Miss Eckhart is imprisoned within a system that pays women poorly for the few skills it lets them learn. She's also asked to believe in the system: to find her poverty appropriate and to see the relatively useless service she provides as worthwhile. In reality, Miss Eckhart's metronome is neither essence nor fetish. It's a device that thinks rhythm for her—just as price thinks value and ideology thinks (feminine) subjectivity. Miss Eckhart, who doesn't count (socially), doesn't *have* to count (musically)—nor can she account for either incapacity. Too bad she can't take her timepiece and blow it all up. Too bad she doesn't have the wherewithal—material as well as mental—to explode the exploitative world we find her in. Although Miss Eckhart, now reduced to agricultural labor, does set fire to the studio apartment she's been forced to leave, she does so not out of feminist rage and class resentment, but to protest her dispossession from an abject situation she can only see as a classy vocation.

Erotic

"Love's Litany," Wilde's name for the discursive basis of that many-splendored thing which makes the world go round, can be wonderful—divine, heroic, enchanting, providential, transcendental.[5] But it can be dreary as well—violent, combative, poisonous, enthralling, tyrannical, sacrificial. Devoted mothers, for example, are abandoned by grown children. Devoted "crystallizers" are disillusioned by imperfect love objects. Witty playwrights are betrayed by litigious paramours. And, thanks to Goethe, Wertheresque lovers—sad, solitary, suicidal—have an especially doleful part to play.

Welty's maiden piano teacher is Wertheresque. Cassie Morrison may love Miss Eckhart, but Miss Eckhart loves Virgie Rainie, a prodigy who doesn't love her back. Can brilliance alone account for the teacher's feelings? Miss Eckhart loves the girl's brutality too ("There was a little weak place in her, vulnerable, and Virgie Rainey found it and showed it to people" [Welty 45]), even though she finds the cathexis indiscriminate ("For Miss Eckhart love was just as arbitrary and one-sided as music teaching" [65]) and useless ("Her love never did anybody any good" [65]) and even though she finds herself alone ("She had nobody at all" [66]). She's grateful, in fact, but her pretentious refrain, "Virgie Rainey, *danke schoen*," leaves us wondering which is the icing and which the cake— brilliance or brutality. According to Cassie, it's the brutality the teacher craves: "It was as though Miss Eckhart, at the last, were grateful to you for *anything*" (73).

Why is Virgie brutal? At first, she resents the way Miss Eckhart imagines her: as an up-and-coming virtuoso, as a gifted pianist who won't have failed. (It's hard to love people who expect too much.) In the end, though, she sees herself as Miss Eckhart: a gifted pianist who *did* fail. Miss Eckhart has already lost her studio. Miss Rainey is about to lose her job as "the piano player at the picture show" (24), a prospect *both* of them should find horrifying. (What teacher wants to know her beloved student has come to naught? What student wants to fail a teacher?)

And yet, to hear Cassie tell it, when the two happen to meet after years of separation, "They did not even horrify each other."

Danke schoen . . . That much was out in the open. Gratitude—like rescue—was simply no more. It was not only past; it was outworn and cast away. Both Miss Eckhart and Virgie Rainey were human beings terribly at large, roaming on the face of the earth. And there were others of them—human beings, roaming, like lost beasts. (96)

Barthesian

Balzac, "Sarrasine" (1830): Marianina de Lanty, a brilliant soprano, bids farewell to La Zambinella, a famous castrato, with an odd little flourish. "'Addio, addio,' she said, with the prettiest inflection in her youthful voice. She added to the final syllable a marvelously well-executed trill, but in a soft voice, as if to give poetic expression to the emotion in her heart" (232–33). According to Barthes, the flourish predicates Marianina as "musical." But—

What would happen if one actually performed Marianina's '*addio*' as it is described in the discourse? Something incongruous, no doubt, extravagant, and not musical. More: is it really possible to perform the act described? This leads to two propositions. The first is that the discourse has no responsibility vis-à-vis the real: in the most realistic novel, the referent has no "reality": suffice it to imagine the disorder the most orderly narrative would create were its descriptions taken at face value, converted into operative programs and simply executed. In short (this is the second proposition), what we call "real" (in the theory of the realistic text) is never more than a code of representation (of signification): it is never a code of execution: *the novelistic real is not operable.* (Barthes, *S/Z* 80)

Kate Chopin, *The Awakening* (1899): Mademoiselle Reisz, a stereotypically unpleasant piano teacher who plays Frédéric Chopin to perfection, does something incredible—and rather seductive—when Edna Pontellier, the lovelorn heroine, wants to hear an Impromptu.

Mademoiselle played a soft interlude. It was an improvisation. She sat low at the instrument, and the lines of her body settled into ungraceful curves and angles that gave it an appearance of deformity. Gradually and imperceptibly the interlude melted into the soft opening minor chords of the Chopin Impromptu.

Edna did not know when the Impromptu began or ended. She sat in the sofa corner reading Robert's letter by the fading light. Mademoiselle had glided from the Chopin into the quivering lovenotes of Isolde's song, and back again to the Impromptu with its soulful and poignant longing.

The shadows deepened in the little room. The music grew strange and fantastic—turbulent, insistent, plaintive, and soft with entreaty. The shadows grew deeper. The music filled the room. It floated out upon the night, over the housetops, the crescent of the river, losing itself in the silence of the upper air.

Edna was sobbing. (527)

There is no such Impromptu. The Chopin Impromptus are in major, and the Fantasie-Impromptu (C-sharp minor) opens with left-hand figuration. And even if the Impromptu did exist, what kind of musician would interpolate the *Liebestod*?

According to Mademoiselle Reisz, and quite possibly according to Kate: a *true* musician. "The artist," she tells Edna, "must possess the courageous soul . . . [t]he soul that dares and defies" (527). Edna does dare and defy, but doesn't do so aesthetically—something she realizes just before she drowns herself: "How Mademoiselle Reisz would have laughed, perhaps sneered, if she knew! 'And you call yourself an artist! What pretensions, Madame!'" (555). ("The natural aversion for water," moreover, is "believed to accompany the artistic temperament" [518]. Who is speaking here? Kate? Edna? Anyone in particular?) Edna defies her husband, refusing to act the wife and mother. But she's both too timid to paint unconventionally (everything she does is "lifelike," or tries to be [522]) and too timid to *live* unconventionally. In other words, she's too bourgeois to face the music. Mademoiselle Reisz, however, does face—and de-face—the music. She, like Barthes, throws caution to the wind, plays paradoxically (yet affectingly), and doesn't give a damn whether people "like" her.[6]

The woman, after all, isn't very *nice*.

Queer

Cassie Morrison knows about Miss Eckhart's metronome, but doesn't know what makes the woman tick. Edna Pontellier knows about her own desire, but not about anyone else's. Fortunately, Welty and Chopin—both Southern *belles lettristes*—may know more than Cassie and Edna. (Most Southern belles know more than they can say.) Where Cassie assumes Miss Eckhart loves Virgie Rainey's brutality, Welty seems to believe the teacher finds the student arousing: "Those two . . . had been making a trip . . . the sailor [Virgie slept with] was only starting" (96). And where Edna assumes Mademoiselle Reisz has "never been in love, and know[s] nothing about it" (536), Chopin seems to realize the teacher is in love with Edna. According to Edna, Mademoiselle Reisz finds "queer" reasons to embrace her: "For instance, when I left her to-day, she put her arms around me and felt my shoulder blades, to see if my wings were strong, she said" (537). (They weren't, making Edna a false Winged Victory.)

Is Kathrine Parker a lesbian? Is she bisexual? Was Rosina Lhevinne? (What *was* all that banging, anyway?) Rumor has it Myra Hess was a lesbian, and I, for one, believe it. Not because I find her playing, or anyone ever found her teaching, lesbianic, but because queer Wayne Koestenbaum claims to be a "descendant" ("Piano Life" l. 123). And because when Hess first saw the true Winged Victory, she was "overwhelmed," spent several hours "drinking it in," and "let it have its way" with her (MacKail 13).

Intermezzo

Sammy Cohen, a moving man who used to work for my father, once tried to impress him by asking Bob, then eleven, to play Ernesto Lecuona's *Malagueña*. My mother considered the request "uncouth," as did Bob, who replied somewhat snobbily, "I don't play *Malagueña*."

Edgar Garza-Morales, a wealthy lawyer I used to work for, once tried to impress me by having his boyfriend, a gifted cocktail pianist, play *Malagueña*. Having never heard the piece played well before, I was impressed. So impressed, in fact, that I thought about learning it. But I didn't. I didn't even buy the score.

I finally bought it yesterday—one of the nervier purchases I've ever made. And when Ozzie Diaz-Duque, a queeny philologist I now work with, had me show him what was in the bag, he exclaimed: "Lecuona! My mother used to be his maid!"

CHAPTER 6

❧ *Classified Information*

Mister Sandman, bring us a dream.
Give him a pair of eyes with a come-hither
  gleam.
Give him a lonely heart like Pa-gli-acci
And lots of wavy hair like Liberace!

Pat Ballard, "Mister Sandman"

❧ I can't recall having dreamt of Liberace. Nothing about him lulls my slumber—the hair, the wink, the smile. The furs. The cars. The beads. The diamonds. The glass instruments. The camp sensibility. The queen mother. The faggy voice. The Paderewskian technique. The Chopinesque candelabra. The Wildean litigation. The gay death. No, not one dream. Not even a nightmare. I do, however, think of Liberace. In fact, I think of him a lot. (An *awful* lot, to mimic Jeffrey Swann.) The man simply haunts—and taunts—my imagination. Or not so simply. Liberace baffles me in ways that, given the ludicrous ease with which he dominated popular (and not so popular) culture, don't go without saying.

Let me pose a few questions. Do you have to be homophobic to hate Liberace? Do you have to be a snob? Do you have to be a "fag hag" to love him? Do you have to be *déclassé*? Can you be a homophobic fag hag? Can you be a déclassé snob? Let me proffer tentative answers. No. No. Yes and no. Yes and no. Yes. And yes. Now let me schematize an attempt to verify them (the questions as well as the answers). What do straight viewers make of Liberace? What do straight listeners make of him? What do gay viewers make of Liberace? What about gay listeners? And what did Liberace make of himself? True, the scheme is problematic. The experience of virtuosity, or pseudo-virtuosity, is both visual and acoustic. It's hard to separate heterosexuals and homosexuals. And it's hard to know how celebrities really see (and hear) themselves. But when you're this baffled, you settle for "problematic."

Liberace appealed to middle-class and lower-class women over 40. He also, and for reasons few have tried to fathom, appealed to their husbands.[1] What did they see in him? Marian Thomas can speak—and speak at length—for some of the women.

Festival Hall began to fill up. We could hardly believe our luck when we were led to two seats in the second row right in front of the black glass-topped piano. Everbody . . . seemed so calm. I wondered if they were in such a turmoil of emotional excitement and impatience as I was.

All at once an ear-shattering roll of drums sounded. . . . "Ladies and gentlemen, Crawford productions have great pride in presenting"—the lights dim—"that man who is famous throughout the world for his candelabra"—a roll of drums—"and his piano"—a blue spotlight flashed upon the stage entrance; all eyes turned to it—"the best dressed man in show business, the star of our show, Mr. Showmanship . . . LIBERACE!"

Finally! He was on stage. I almost breathed a sigh of relief. For the duration of approximately three seconds total silence reigned, and then such a thunderous applause rose that, while gazing at him, I pictured the roof lifting off with the sheer pressure of the sound.

From the moment he walked before the mass of people he had one and all in the palm of his hand. Sighs and gasps could be heard. Dressed in full-length maxi blue coat, fur trimmed with solid gold epaulets, overflowing with happiness and personality, he could be described as nothing less than spectacular. With "a smile as wide as his piano keyboard" he bowed and walked across the stage, waiting until he could be heard above the tremendous ovation. When, at last, we ceased clapping (mainly due to rather sore hands) he launched into the type of jokes that have become so much a part of his act, so well known by anyone who has any interest in Liberace, and yet which were still so humorous when he delivered them. "Well. Look me over. I didn't get dressed like this to go unnoticed. Do you like this one?" We did, of course. We'd love him in anything. "It was made for me when I had the honour to play a Royal Command Performance, and would you believe it, out of all the performers there, I was the only person with one like it!" Not impossible to believe. Taking this off, he revealed a golden waistcoat and white, puffed-lace pantaloons. After recovering from this outfit, he asked, "Well, are you ready for music?" What a question! Amid still more sighs and the voice of a woman behind me murmuring, "He's too good to be true," (I agreed entirely) he infused his amazing musical ability into the beautiful melodies of "Theme From Love Story," "Raindrops Keep Falling on My Head," "Close to You," following these contemporary tunes with the masterpieces of the great composer Chopin.

One could hear a pin drop in that theater. He then relinquished the stage to a young boy of ten years; the youngest professional juggler in the world. I don't know if Liberace needed the rest but I certainly did. I was feeling emotionally pulverized.

However, Liberace rushed back within five minutes in an outfit of pink silk with a jacket made of a thousand little mirrors, all of which dazzled the eyes as they reflected the light of his candelabra all around the building. Then Liberace virtually achieved the impossible—he bridged the generation gap by swinging into a medley from *Hair* to the enjoyment of all ages. He refused to play it in the nude . . . judging by the number of unhappy "ohs" this seemed rather a disappointment to some people. So after sending us through the universe to the star Aquarius, he played and narrated "The Impossible Dream"—the song by which he wished to be remembered. I'll remember him by it and every time I hear a lovely piece of music, or hear the note of a piano, I'll remember him. . . .

Two costume changes later, after playing everything from boogie-woogie in double time to a Gershwin medley, he announced the end of the show. We thought differently. Amid the cries of 8,000 anguished fans yelling for "more" he decided to give it to us, as he "was in no hurry to go if we weren't." We weren't. In fact, we would just not let him go.

A thrill swept through the audience when Liberace bent over the stage, showing his fabulous rings, and inspecting those of others. He played seven encores on demand, his last being a beautiful song called "Ciao," one which was most appropriate, to say good-bye. Many tears could be discovered in many eyes. The lights dimmed for the last time as he switched off his candelabra. But with Liberace there had to be a spectacular ending to a truly spectacular show. In complete darkness, suddenly his suit lit up so that he resembled a miniature Christmas tree. The lights then blazed on, revealing Lee on stage laughing and every member of the audience giving him a thundering, standing ovation.

We rushed to the stage to shake his hand and after a few bows, winks, smiles and waves, suddenly, like a breath of magic he was gone, taking a little part of Melbourne with him. We all sat down again, reluctant to move. It took an hour to fully clear the hall. (Liberace, *Autobiography* 296–99)

Liberace, for these women, is quite a sight. He's a "radiant" vision of love, a "spectacular" vision of wealth ("solid gold epaulets"), class ("royal" connections), skill ("amazing ability"), culture (Chopin "masterpieces"), and *niceness*.[2] He's just "too good to be true"—and is especially good to his mother, the one woman to whom Liberace was, in fact, unabashedly devoted. (Filial devotion, which Thomas fails to mention, was central to the act.) But even though he's a "glitzy object of the [female] gaze" (Drewal 173), he isn't a particularly sexy one. Like Louis Jourdan in *Letter from an Unknown Woman*, but for reasons relating to a proximity to Chopin (his "favorite" composer)[3] and to what Marjorie Garber calls an "unmarked transvestism" (354),[4] and not for ones relating to heterosexual promiscuity,[5] Liberace is rather effeminate. And unlike Rock Hudson, a clean-cut matinee idol female fans *did* undress with their eyes, Liberace never packaged himself in ways that made many women want to see him nude.[6]

Thomas, to me, seems déclassé. She seems to lack cultural capital, or "taste"—to admire Liberace's "ability" because she hasn't been exposed to good pianism and, like him, to equate Chopin and Gershwin. She even calls a constellation a "star." But is the woman a "fag hag"—a demeaning stereotype I'll try to transvalue? (Think of "hag" as Mary Daly does. Think of "fag" as you choose.) According to some, she can't see Liberace as faggy even though she can see him as effeminate. For Margaret Drewal, for example, "an overt homosexual identity would have been unacceptable to Liberace's blue-collar, heterosexual, and homophobic audiences, who preferred *not* to view him as gay, but instead focussed on his devotion to his mother, an image that Liberace himself promoted" (150). Michael Thompson calls this heterosexual preference a "conspiracy of blindness" (2). David Bergman calls it "The Liberace Effect"—"to be so exaggerated an example of what you in fact are that people think you couldn't possibly be it" (14).[7] However, it's possible Liberace lovers knew he was gay—just as they knew their favorite hairdressers and (less déclassé) decorators were. It's also possible they liked the fact that he was gay. It meant they had a man they could talk to, if only in their dreams—an intimate associate who engaged in conversations their husbands weren't keen on, but who wouldn't prove to be a sexual "threat." For homophilic female fans, then, Liberace was a nonsexual lover, whereas for homophobic fans he was a presexual, or infantile, one—one they, too, could mother.

Or so they say—"they" meaning people other than Liberace's female fans. When Diane Wakoski wonders why her homophilic mother, and even she herself, likes Liberace, he comes across as *post*-sexual. To let the woman speak for herself, yet again at length (excuse the excess—I'm not quite used to doing so):

> The diamond grand,
> its lid upraised,
> the diamond butterfly,
> the diamonds of South African mines,
> clasping his fingers,
> one for every tour, one ring for
> his fortieth anniversary
> in show business, all sitting
> as if they were in howdahs, above his
> fingers,
> which continue to move as if
> utterly
> unencumbered. Not elephants but manatees
> swimming in the Crystal River,
> glissandos,
> arpeggios, weaving hands, moving
> like dragonflies
> though they resemble hod-carriers
> more, with the diamond-loads,
> an effort of masonry.
>
> What does it mean
> never to get tired
> of playing "Jingle Bells" or Chopin,
> to have a chandelier
> in your greenhouse,
> or piano keyboard painted on the door
> of one of your limousines,

to love men,
to wear silly shirts,
to have millions of pathetic old women
in love with you
   my mother:
     yr only rival with her—
  Lawrence Welk.

Why am I, the girl who gave up
the piano
to make meaning out of her life,
who never watches television,
does not own a tv set,
watching with such seriousness
this talk show
with Liberace telling about
each diamond ring he wears?
Why
thinking with admiration
of his skill, equal to most
great pianists?
       Why
am I wishing
for as much shape and purpose
from any such burden of diamonds
and tinkling keys?

Why do so many of us admire,
long for,
men who only love other men?

Do we need betrayers
and denyers
to reinforce our own failures?
Or are we searching for
some final answer,
beyond the greater measure,
beyond sex,
beyond our own mortality?[8]

I can't call Wakoski déclassé, even though she, too, admires Liberace's ability ("skill equal to most great pianists"). She claims to know good playing from bad ("You were the piano prodigy, / and I, untalented, / the one who wanted to play" ["Beautiful" ll. 66–68]). She prefers classical music to popular ("I do not know 'Stella By Starlight' but I know Chopin" ["Virtuoso Literature" pt. II, l. 60]). She's a poet. And she hates television, the medium that made "Liberace" a household name. But neither are the Wakoskis stereotypical fag hags. Stereotypically "pathetic" hags do "need betrayers / and deniers / to reinforce [their] own failures," and hence underscore a homophobic equation of homosexuality and inadequacy (if not the late modern figuration of homosexuality as an imitation of heterosexuality, or as an arrested development, then the early modern figuration of homosexuality as treasonous [*self*-betrayal]).[9] For these two, however, Liberace represents *Liebestod*—a "final answer . . . beyond sex, beyond . . . mortality." He plays Tristan (another feminized romantic) to their Isolde, or Isolde to their Tristan. After all, it's Liberace who's doing all the singing.

He also plays loving vampire to their willing victim. Contrary to the popular belief Bram Stoker fostered, most nineteenth-century vampires resembled Liberace. Unlike Dracula, that is, they were both effeminate and friendly. Liberace himself understood the connection, flitting about in capes that reminded fans of Bela Lugosi, or of Bela Lugosi as Dracula,[10] and portraying a "prissy" undertaker who sleeps in a coffin in Tony Richardson's *The Loved One* (1965).[11] But he probably didn't understand the connection between vampirism and homoeroticism. "To comprehend the vampire," writes *un*friendly Ellis Hanson, "is to recognize that abjected space that gay men are obliged to inhabit. [The gay man is] the caped one, who hovers over the dreaming body of Jonathan Harker and exclaims, 'This man belongs to me!' and 'Yes, I too can love'" (325). Did Liberace's female fans understand this second connection? For example, did the hags he took "beyond mortality" simply see themselves as Lucy Westenra—as women he did threaten (in a *nice* way)? Or did they try to see themselves as Jonathan Harker—as men he did in fact prefer? "What does it mean [for Liberace] to love men?" Only a man would know for sure.

A hairdresser would know, of course. But what about a husband? Why did Liberace appeal to fans' husbands? Why did these men enjoy the show? Some saw it the way their wives did—as a classy, and classic, vicarious thrill. They appreciated the spectacle of material wealth they knew they would never attain and musical taste they thought they had attained.[12] In other words, they liked Liberace the way they liked Elvis, who managed to replicate several features of the pianist's showy style (the cape, the glitter, the filial devotion) without appearing quite so queer.[13] These men thought that Liberace represented great Romantic pianism, even though he was worse than Paderewski (an early "idol"), and that Elvis represented great rhythm and blues, even though he was worse than the African-American singers he tried to imitate (Muddy Waters, Rufus Thomas, Jackie Wilson)—proving that one can be déclassé in relation to both popular and nonpopular culture.[14]

Were some of the husbands fag hags? It's a startling suggestion, but there is such a thing as a male fag hag. Like the female fag hag, the male fag hag (or "fruit fly") is dazzled by the degree to which gay men evade heterosexual masculinity—a construction both of them find constrictive. For the male hag, however, the experience is completely vicarious. Whereas a woman can't quite see herself as a liberated man,[15] a man can.

Ordinarily, this should make him very nervous, because few
married men care to think they might be sodomitical, and
could even turn him into the kind of "fag" his wife would like
to "hag"—if, that is, she's the type of "woman (don't we all
know them?) who has not only the most delicate nose for but
the most potent attraction toward men who are at crises of
homosexual panic [and who finds] that an arousing nimbus,
an excessively refluent and dangerous maelstrom of eroticism,
somehow attends men in general at such moments, even otherwise boring men" (Sedgwick, *Epistemology* 209). Thank God,
then, Liberace has two non-sexualities. One for homophilic
female fag hags, who don't wish to be put upon and to whom
he seems like a nonthreatening non-*hetero*sexual. And one for
homophobic male fag hags, who don't wish to have their heterosexuality called into question (and hence are relatively ret-
icent about their love of Liberace) and to whom he seems like
a nonthreatening non-*homo*sexual—or at least like a nonthreatening non-*practicing* homosexual. On the other hand,
thank God some of the husbands, who given the pandemic
incidence of homosexual panic are really rather extraordinary,
could look into Liberace's (glass) closet, see that they inhabit
one as well, and decide to step out and "get busy."

What do nongay *listeners* make of Liberace? Some have a
camp sensibility and love the fact that he's a bad pianist. These,
however, aren't exactly fans of Florence Foster Jenkins, the terrible coloratura soprano who, unlike Liberace, took herself
very seriously and hence appealed to an audience that appreciated "naive" camp.[16] Other listeners hate the fact that he's a
bad pianist—or hate the fact that people think he plays classical music and think he plays it well. They can't stand Liberace's technical disability—the sloppy fingering, the puerile
pedaling. Liberace, notes the *New York Herald Tribune*, "plays

[the] piano as if he were wearing boxing gloves" (Thomas 81). "Pedal work difficult to analyze," states the *New Yorker*. "Keeps pumping feet up and down and sidewise, as though he were on an electric horse" (Thomas 89). Nor can the listeners stand his artistic incompetence. Liberace, according to the London *Times*, "play[s] the piano quite unmusically and often in de-plorable taste" (Thomas 121). They hate both the glittery pas-sagework (even when he does carry it off) and the effeminate sentimentality. "[The] sentimentally exaggerated retards and accellerandos," notes the *New York Times* after the Carnegie Hall debut, "[indicate] a type of piano playing frequently heard in cocktail lounges" (Thomas 80). "What kind of pianist is Liberace," it wonders about the recordings, which are purely auditory:

Don't ask a square with Horowitz and Rubinstein on the brain. He'll say that Liberace is not much more than a parlor pianist who ought to be kept in someone else's parlor. Such a bilious critic will point out a lot of flaws—slackness of rhythm, distorted phrasing, and an excess of prettification and sentimentality, a failure to stick to what the composer has written. (Thomas 82)

Liberace fails to regard what composers have written in other ways as well. He both belittles and bastardizes music campy listeners no longer care for, but classy ones do. He con-denses scores they still know and love, making "Reader's Di-gest versions" of the "Minute" Waltz, which he plays in half a minute, and the "Moonlight" Sonata, which he plays in three. (Unlike Horowitz, Liberace is a true miniaturist, a musician of whom Barthes would not have written: "I hear it said [he played] short pieces *because he didn't know how to develop*. A repressive criticism: what you *refuse* to do is what you can't do" ["Rasch" 300].) The trick, Liberace claims, is "cutting out the dull parts." With Tchaikovsky, for example, "I play his

melodies and skip his spiritual struggles" (Thomas 66, 67).
He also adulterates classical music, turning a Hungarian Rhap-
sody into "Chopsticks" and the "Aeolian Harp" Etude into
"Sincerely Yours," a theme song. The piano teacher in Kate
Chopin's *The Awakening* pulls a similar stunt, of course. But
whereas Mademoiselle Reisz Wagnerizes Chopin, which Edna
Pontellier finds aesthetic, Liberace popularizes him, which
many listeners, myself included, find rather mortifying.

In other words, snobby listeners hate Liberace because he's
middlebrow. Just as literati loathe the way Reader's Digest
turns novels into pabulum (and even loathe the way Book-of-
the-Month Club mass markets them),[17] musical connoisseurs
loathe the way Liberace encroaches on their field of expertise.
Some, of course, dislike popular, or lowbrow, music just as
much. They hate Elvis as much as they hate Liberace, and not
because the two dress alike. Others, however, like popular music. If conventional, they may like the music *and* the fact that
it can't claim to be serious. And if relatively unconventional—
if, for example, they appreciate cultural critics who find Elvis,
or Madonna, "revolutionary"—they may like the music and
the fact that it *can* claim to be subversive. As long as it doesn't
undermine, or degrade, the classical music they rarely find
equally revolutionary. As long, that is, as the music doesn't
disturb the distinction between highbrow and lowbrow—
which, of course, is what middlebrow culture, including middlebrow music, does do.

This, then, is what bothered the critics who had Liberace
"crying all the way to the bank." They resented his technical
disability, his musical incompetence, and his middlebrow orientation. Other critics, ones with eyes as well as ears, hated
him because they were homophobic—and had him hauling
them into court. Oscar Wilde brought a highly publicized li-

bel action against the (illiterate) Marquess of Queensberry, who had accused him of "posing as a somdomite," and lost. Truth, after all, isn't defamatory. Liberace brought one against *Confidential*, which suggested that his "theme song should be 'Mad About the Boy,'" and settled. He also brought one against the *Daily Mirror*, a British tabloid—and won. The *Mirror* text, like those of Thomas and Wakoski, bears quoting at length:

He is the summit of sex—the pinnacle of masculine, feminine and neuter. Everything that he, she and it can ever want.

I spoke to sad but kindly men on this newspaper who have met every celebrity arriving from the United States for the past 30 years. They say that this deadly, winking, sniggering, snuggling, chromium-plated, scent-impregnated, luminous, quivering, giggling, fruit-flavored, mincing, ice-covered heap of mother love has had the biggest reception and impact on London since Charlie Chaplin arrived at the same station, Waterloo, on September 12, 1921.

This appalling man—and I use the word appalling in no other than its true sense of terrifying—has hit this country in a way that is as violent as Churchill receiving the cheers on V-E Day.

He reeks with emetic language that can only make grown men long for a quiet corner, an aspidistra, a handkerchief, and the old heave-ho. Without doubt he is the biggest sentimental vomit of all times. Slobbering over his mother, winking at his brother, counting the cash at every second, this superb piece of calculating candy-floss has an answer for every situation. . . .

Nobody since Aimee Semple MacPherson has purveyed a bigger, richer and more varied slag-heap of lilac-covered hokum. Nobody anywhere made so much money out of high-speed piano playing with the ghost of Chopin gibbering at every note. (Thomas 121–22)

I find this quite as appalling as it claims to find Liberace. I also find it rather appealing—to the residual snob in me, if not to the residual homophobe. It can be hard to separate the two—as "Cassandra" himself (William Neil Connor, the author of the article) should have realized. Men like Gide, Bar-

thes, and Liberace—queer pianists, but opera queens and in-
terior decorators as well—simulate the taste of an upper class
that hates their homosexuality and so can't afford to incorporate them.[18] It can, however, afford to disparage them and
to associate the bad imitation of taste with the bad imitation
of heterosexuality. Cassandra, for example, finds Liberace's
playing both mortifying ("the ghost of Chopin gibbering at
every note") and "lilac-covered." (I presume he wouldn't find
Rubinstein's Chopin so—and that he would find Gide's.) The
class can even afford to *pay* for having disparaged them—in
this case twenty thousand dollars in damages and forty thousand in costs. The jury, as usual, having been treated to several spectacular denials, two of which were false—Cassandra
refusing to acknowledge his homophobia (the phrase "masculine, feminine and neuter," he claimed, indicated Liberace's
"comprehensive" sex appeal [Thomas 140], a rather disin-
genuous anticipation of Wakoski's poetic, "beyond sex"); Liberace refusing to acknowledge either his "comprehensive" sexuality ("I could hardly refer to myself as a sexy performer"
[Thomas 133]) or his homosexuality—chose to follow its own
class interests, which it found reflected in the performer, and
not in the *Mirror*. One woman juror, moments before the de-
livery of the guilty verdict, even went so far as to wink (back?)
at Liberace and mouth the words, "It's all right" (Thomas 145).

What do gay viewers make of Liberace? (I can neither speak
for Liberace's lesbian fans nor have them speak for themselves.
Did he, in fact, *have* any?) Pre-Stonewall gays enjoyed peering into his glass closet, much as Proustians enjoy peering into
that of Charlus. They delighted in a gay spectacle, in a sexual
knowledge the subject himself didn't seem to possess, and in
a diversion of attention away from their own closets.[19] Noel
Coward, for example, having met Liberace aboard the *Queen*

Mary, paid him a compliment that spoke to this complicated—and self-implicating—pleasure. "I've seen your act," he said. "You do what you do *very* well" (Thomas 119). And what he did, more or less deliberately, was package himself for muffled gay consumption as well as for middlebrow mass consumption. Post-Stonewall gays who can afford to be out are far less complimentary. They see Liberace as both unliberated and undesirable. They loathe him not because they're homophobic, but because *he's* homophobic. They hate him for having denied his homosexuality, and the fact that he had AIDS, until the day he died—something even Rock Hudson didn't do. To cite The Flirtations' version of "Mister Sandman":

> Mister Sandman, bring me a dream.
> Please make him gargle and brush with Gleem.
> Give him a lonely heart like Pa-gli-acci,
> But not as closeted as Liberace![20]

Snobby gay listeners, of course, aren't much nicer. They may not hate what Liberace does to himself, but they do hate what he does to Chopin. Campy gay listeners, however, are relatively kind. Like their non-gay counterparts, they appreciate the bad playing, as well as the belittlement and bastardization of classical music. Or, to be fair to camp sensibilities, they appreciate Liberace's (modern) celebration of technical failure, as well as the flair with which he breathes new life—and new significance—into music only purists find worth preserving. Whereas postmodern camp (John Boskovich's *Without You I'm Nothing* [1990], Jennie Livingston's *Paris Is Burning* [1992]) values profundity, sobriety, sincerity, and talent, modern camp (Oscar Wilde, John Waters) values surface over depth, playfulness over seriousness, artificiality over authenticity, and ineptitude over aptitude. And whereas some camp acts (Florence

Foster Jenkins, for example) can be called naive and taken as failed seriousness, Liberace can be called Barthesian, because he (re)produced dated texts non-campy snobs continue to consume. "Experiencing the camp glow," Koestenbaum writes, "is a way of reversing one's abjection and, by witnessing the depletion of cultural monuments, experiencing one's own power to fill degraded artifacts to the brim with meanings" (*Queen's Throat* 117). *Flirtations* fans experience that glow whenever they hear the new "Mister Sandman." Campy Liberace fans experience it whenever they hear "Sincerely Yours."

Some campy fans take things even further, and applaud Liberace's middlebrow demolition of the highbrow/lowbrow distinction. According to Margaret Drewal, who attended a Radio City Music Hall appearance:

Liberace told the audience that many classical pieces have been turned into popular tunes, but what he wanted to do was to turn popular tunes, like "Mack the Knife," into the classics, suggesting further that this is what the "classic" composers would do if they could have their revenge. Even suggesting that a classical composer would want to turn a popular song into a classical one is a curious reversal. In truth "Mack the Knife" is a popularized song derived from Bertolt Brecht's *The Threepenny Opera*, music by Kurt Weill, itself based on John Gay's *The Beggar's Opera*. In essence, Liberace was deconstructing hierarchically structured categories. First, he played it "straight." Then he played "Mack the Knife Sonata in C Major" by Mozart, "Claire de Lune de Mack the Knife" by Debussy, and finally "Blue Mack the Knife Danube" by Strauss. In elevating a pop tune to the status of classical music, or so he would have it, he simultaneously highlighted the impact of style on content. Playing "Mack the Knife" straight before totally transforming it commented on the absurd way in which the categories themselves, which are human constructs, operate to organize attitudes and taste. (155)

Liberace, of course, had mastered the "deconstructive" transcription, which Ivan Raykoff, echoing Drewal, characterizes

as a "transgressive, counterhegemonic, [and] subversive treatment of [a] musical text," quite early in his career. He earned
his first major headline ("Three Little Fishies Swim in a Sea
of Classics") by improvising Mozartian, Beethovenian, and
Chopinesque variations on a Kay Kyser novelty number ("Fim,
little fishies, fim if you can") (Thomas 28). Like the critics who
find Madonna revolutionary, however, Drewal and Raykoff
are far too sanguine. For one thing, the people who'd truly
benefit from Liberace's deconstructive (or middlebrow) magic
—ones devoted to classical music and hence over-invested in
cultural capital—aren't likely to find themselves in his audience. Drewal isn't classically oriented, or so I gather from her
déclassé notion that Paderewski was a "violinist" (Drewal 177).
Raykoff is, but attends to Liberace only for the sake of argument—as do I. For another, classical music lovers who find
themselves in the audience know of an antideconstructive
charm. Liberace, they can tell themselves, is simply idiosyncratic. To cite the *New York Times* reading of the appearance
Drewal finds subversive, "Liberace has arrived at a style that
is not classical, jazz or pop but an ornamental genre unto itself. . . . [He is] a one-of-a-kind musical monument" (Thomas
239).

Oddly enough, campy critics don't applaud every aspect of
Liberace's modern superficiality. Queer theorists who, working in the wake of Judith Butler, privilege professional female,
and professional male, impersonation when discussing the artificiality of gender and sexuality—who have "women" like
Mae West and "Divine" (Glenn Milstead) enact heterosexual
femininity and "men" like Rudolph Valentino and "Octavian"
(in *Der Rosenkavalier*) enact heterosexual masculinity—never
mention "Mr. Showmanship."[21] Like Drewal, they hear Liberace's musical style ("In elevating a pop tune to the status of

classical music, [he] highlighted the impact of style on content"), but fail to see his non-musical ones. They fail, that is, to recognize the way he, too, underscored the "performativity" of gender and sexuality—and class. The failure, no doubt, is due to the fact that Liberace's transvestism is relatively "unmarked." But it's also due to the fact that he didn't *do* these identities very well. Like early Proust, he was an amateur aristocrat. Like early Gide, he was an amateur heterosexual. Like late Barthes, he was an amateur homosexual. And if there's one person professional theorists (other than Koestenbaum) have yet to appreciate, it's the amateur.

What did Liberace make of himself? Once again, it's hard to know. Liberace was a celebrity and as a celebrity peddled self-promoting stories, most of which were false. In fact, the whole point of celebrity may be "the spectacle of people forced to tell transparent lies in public" (Moon and Sedgwick 25). Lies like, "I happen to be secure in my masculinity" and "I'm taking my time looking for the right woman." But he was a diva as well. And divas as "performative" as Liberace—divas, that is, who never wonder, "If we do 'perform' ourselves, who's doing the performing?"—tend to, or seem to, believe their lies.[22] Whereas Mae West situated her true self as nonperformative, Liberace situated himself as truly theatrical—which would make Liberace a Wildean forebear of Butler, an anti-essentialist *avant la lettre* (or *malgré lui*), and West a Gidean forebear of Butler's crypto-essentialist critics. To cite the opening pages of the autobiography he did, in fact, write himself:

I've discovered that every performer—and I've known most of them in my time—is really two distinctly different people. I was first made aware of this several years ago, when [Mae West] told me the fascinating story of her life. I noticed she always spoke of herself in the third person, referring to Mae West as if she wasn't present. It didn't take me long to realize I actually wasn't with the world's greatest sex symbol. That Mae West was a self-creation who had captured the public's attention and become a legend never to be surpassed. She had made the word "sex" synonymous with "fun" and never "dirty." But the person [I was with] was a sweet and dignified lady who did not drink, or smoke, or utter a single naughty word.

I find it equally natural to speak of "Mr. Showmanship" Liberace as if he were another person. The man behind the music, the glamour, the glitz, the man who has created a successful career spanning more than forty years, is another Liberace. He's the one you're going to meet in this book. . . .

So here it is, a very personal letter from me to you, sharing an intimate glimpse into the wonderful private world of Liberace. (*Wonderful Private World* 7–8).

Note the implicit italics, and the inadvertent slippage between the first and third persons. We don't get a glimpse into "my private world," but a glimpse into "*the wonderful private world of* LIBERACE." Nor do we read about the gay man behind the music. We (re)read the nongay legend up in which Liberace "himself" gets caught.

So which of Liberace's stories—and in particular the stories that concern his desirous identifications, or cathexes—were true? Which were false? And which of them did he believe? For someone with so many "idols," Liberace paid a lot of lip service to self-generation. He, too, made use of the antideconstructive charm. "I can honestly say," he lied, "I know of no one who does the same thing I do, good or bad, in the same way I do it, which puts me in a class all by myself" (*Autobiography* 85–86). But he didn't use the charm to ward off middlebrow magic. He used it to ward off the feeling of failure. He even claimed it did the trick, for which, like Phyllis Diller, he credited Claude Bristol's *The Magic of Believing* (1948), the popular self-help manual that first had him looking into mirrors and reciting similar and equally charming "affirmations." But I doubt it did. For one thing, every such affirmation represents a denial (*omnis determinatio negatio est*)—a matter of common, as well as deconstructive, sense. (Just ask "Stuart Smalley" [Al Franken], who, in *I'm Good Enough, I'm Smart Enough, and Doggone It, People Like Me!*, parodies *The Magic of Believing* to perfection.) Diller, for example, continued making fun of her appearance even after having read Bristol's book and even after the face lifts that, to quote "'Dame' Edna Everage" (Barry Humphries), probably left the small of her back looking like a Brussels sprout. For another, Liberace did realize he hadn't measured up to some of the people he idolized—and probably realized he hadn't measured up to the others, either. Or all but one of the others.

To begin with primal figures, Liberace knew he never satisfied his father, a French-horn player who saw the boy as a concert pianist. "I never became the kind of musician Dad wanted me to be" (*Autobiography* 114), he admits, which may explain why he had so little to do with the man. And he probably knew he never satisfied his mother—which may explain why he did so much for her. Even though she basked in the glow of her middle son's middlebrow success, the woman loathed the thought—or notion—of his homosexuality. "[My mother] is extremely proud of her children," Liberace testified at the British trial, "perhaps a bit more proud of me" (Thomas 132). Yet she was both sickened by what she'd read about Liberace in the paper, a psychosomatic illness that prompted him to sue, and wary of the young men who hung about the Sherman Oaks house, a homophobic suspicion he couldn't quite confirm. "I don't like those hillbillies," she complained. "Get rid of them." "Oh, Mom," Liberace replied. "They relax me. It's the only time I can just be myself" (Thomas 125).

He "idolized" the Queen Mother as well (*Autobiography* 186) and did so in a way that informs the camp appreciation both "Buddy Cole" (Scott Thompson, one of *The Kids in the Hall*) and Dame Edna satirize. (Buddy is a barfly and Edna a housewife who think of themselves as close to the Royal Family. In one pointedly class-conscious bit, for example, Edna claims to have taught Queen Elizabeth how to carry a purse.) According to Liberace:

[The Family] are the kind of people I respect most deeply. I respect what they represent and admire the way they go about representing it, [f]or they inject beauty and pageantry into the lives of those who yearn for something better . . . those who can only dream. It's showmanship of a very high order. The changing of the guard, the Beefeaters' old uniforms, the velvet, the fur-trimmed robes of state, the impractical but luxurious quality of everything . . . the gold. (*Autobiography* 156, ellipses in original)

Pianists, of course, have been cultivating royal connections and claiming aristocratic pedigrees for quite some time. Chopin did. So did Liszt and Thalberg. Liberace, however, may be the first to articulate the basic futility of the moves. For one thing, the Royal Family "represent" the real thing—real pageantry, real luxury. Sherman Oaks, after all, is a far cry from Sherwood Forest. For another, neither the Queen nor the Queen Mother is really his friend—and everyone, including Liberace, knows it. "I have offered [my Palm Springs home] to some of my international friends including Queen Elizabeth and Princess Margaret anytime they want to sneak away and take a look at how things are in the colonies," he writes. "It's fun to shut my eyes and picture myself walking into any store in Palm Springs and saying, 'Hi, Harry. I want you to meet my house guest, The Queen of England'" (*Autobiography* 270). Dream on, Lee.

Florence Bettray-Kelly, Liberace's only piano teacher, was another mother figure. Or father figure. Liberace also betrayed Bettray-Kelly by failing to become a classical musician. "She liked me," he wrote, "although my career didn't turn out exactly the way she had in mind" (*Autobiography* 16). But whereas Virgie Rainey, in Welty's "June Recital," spurns Miss Eckhart for having failed her (playing at the picture show, instead of concertizing), and whereas Liberace may have distanced himself from his father for similar reasons, he neither spurned nor distanced himself from his former taskmistress. He remained as devoted to Bettray-Kelly as to his mother. He'd have her coach him from time to time, long after he needed to worry about the poor quality of his playing. He even came around to playing Liszt's *Forest Murmurs*, twenty years after he'd refused to learn it ("It's a stupid piece, and I hate it!"), describing it to his television audience as "my favorite piano number" (Thomas 11–12). An odd choice of words, given that Chopin was his "favorite" composer. Perhaps the differential treatment can be ascribed to Liberace's early knowledge of Bettray-Kelly as somewhat middlebrow herself. After all, they both played popular music on the same Milwaukee radio station, and at more or less the same time.[23] On the other hand, Liberace's father, unlike Virgie Rainey, was an *orchestral* player at the picture show—relatively highbrow work of which he was somewhat proud. He also played for John Philip Sousa—upper middlebrow work of which both he and Liberace were proud as well. "This is something very special to me," the son, holding a highly polished horn, declared at the opening of the Liberace Museum in Las Vegas. "This was my father's. He played it in Sousa's band, and he died at the age of ninety-two" (Thomas 204). If Liszt and Chopin, father and brother, are one man to me, Liszt and Chopin, father and *mother*, are one woman to Liberace—Bettray-Kelly.

Liberace told two self-involved, and rather incredible, stories about Chopin. He claimed to have a piano "once owned by Chopin" (*Autobiography* 262), even though he knew Chopin never owned the instrument and even though he knew Chopin probably never played it. Liberace also claimed to have fetishized candelabra after seeing *A Song to Remember*. "In 1945," he writes, "I saw . . . Cornel Wilde in a movie about the life of Frédéric Chopin, [noticed he] had a candelabra [sic] on the piano, [and] said to myself, 'If candles make Chopin play that well, I'll have candles on my piano'" (*Autobiography* 90). But he must have known that candles didn't do the trick and that he didn't play as well as Chopin—or Cornel Wilde or José Iturbi, who made the sound track. In other words, Liberace's Chopinesque cathexis was disturbingly problematic, as can be seen in the film that tried, but failed, to turn him into a matinee idol—into a Cornel Wilde or, believe it or not, Rudolph Valentino. For in *Sincerely Yours* (1955), Liberace plays "Anthony Warrin," a semi-popular concert pianist who loses his hearing while performing the Polonaise that inspired *Funérailles*—and skips the famous left-hand octaves. It's an omission that signifies Warrin's aural disability, of course. He needs to get off the stage as quickly as possible. But it's also one that signifies Liberace's digital disability, because he probably knew he couldn't handle the passage.

Rudolph Valentino? Liberace had wanted to be a matinee idol and joked about having been a *television* matinee idol, because he yearned to be—or yearned for—his "namesake" (Thomas 100). It was a feeling he could attribute to his starstruck mother, who did, in fact, christen him Wladziu ("Walter") Valentino. As with the "Chopin" piano and Chopinesque candelabra, Liberace publicized this private fixation, placing Valentino's bed in a guest room and silver goblets said to have been wedding gifts to Valentino and Pola Negri in the Liberace Museum. He even copied some of Valentino's costumes. Garber calls Valentino "an unlikely role model," but finds the fixation rather fitting, because both men were unmarked transvestites and readable as gay (Garber 363). Liberace, however, probably didn't find it so, even though he, too, may have done that reading. Unmarked transvestism is "more seductive than explicit 'female impersonation,' which is often designed to confront, scandalize, titillate, or shock" (Garber 354), but Liberace, as he had to realize, was less seductive than Valentino. And after the box office failure of *Sincerely Yours*, he even had to realize that he was less seductive than Louis Jourdan, let alone Cornel Wilde. "I have passed the age where I could be cast as a handsome leading man," he commented—quasi-campily—late in life, "and even when I was *at* that age the idea never occurred to anyone" (*Autobiography* 109).

Liberace also cathected sets of musical celebrities, one of which is polarized along musical lines and one of which, as we've seen, is polarized along sexual lines. "When I was a little kid," he'd tell his Las Vegas audience, "I wanted to be like the concert pianist Paderewski, and then as I grew older the popular pianist Eddy Duchin became my idol" (*Liberace in Las Vegas*). Despite the chronology, however, and despite the eventual preference for popular music the chronology is meant to indicate, Duchin is far less central to "the legend of Liberace." Whereas Liberace, shortly after having "idolized" him, had turned down the opportunity to lead Duchin's band, saying, "I don't want to be another Eddy" (Thomas 34), he was constantly trying to be another Ignaz. He, too, used a single stage name, citing Paderewski, his "favorite" pianist (*Autobiography* 63), as precedent.[24] He, too, played Madison Square Garden, saying they were the only pianists to have done so. He, too, cultivated capillary devotion. (Paderewski had "glorious" shoulder-length hair Harold Schonberg describes as "reddish-blond, thick, and lustrous" [*Virtuosi* 216]. Liberace had equally thick hair "Mister Sandman" calls wavy.) He did an act, called "Playing Duets with the Masters," in which he imitated Paderewski—as well as Horowitz, Rubinstein, and Iturbi.[25] He had "Anthony Warrin," in *Sincerely Yours*, play Paderewski's Carnegie Hall debut piano. And like Liszt, who came to believe in the spurious *Weihekuss*, he even claimed to have received Paderewski's musical consecration. Paderewski, so the story goes, heard Liberace, then eight, play Chopin, patted the boy on the head (a kiss, by then, would have been a bit much), and said, "Some day this boy may take my place" (Thomas 7). Unfortunately, Liberace didn't take his place. Even though both pianists enjoyed immense popularity and even though both of them were discredited by cognoscenti,[26] only Paderewski played seriously enough, and well enough, to enter the classical music pantheon.

The celebrities polarized along sexual lines are, of course, Horowitz and Rubinstein. Not only did Liberace reincarnate the two of them in "Playing Duets with the Masters," he incorporated them in magical "affirmations" as well. He is said to have gazed into mirrors, asking, "Liberace, are you as good a pianist as Horowitz?" and answering, "No, but I'm probably better than him in some regards" (Thomas 74). And he loved to tell people, "Liberace is no Rubinstein, but then, neither is Rubinstein any Liberace"—a favorite quip to which he would add the occasional tag, "I'll bet Rubinstein is glad, [but] I'd like to be both of us" (*Autobiography* 102). Every affirmation, after all, represents a denial. Paradoxically enough, or not, the Horowitz reflection ("I'm somewhat better than Horowitz") is belied by the Rubinstein affirmation ("I want to be Rubinstein, but Rubinstein doesn't want to be me"). Paradoxical, because one expects public affirmations to be belied by private reflections. Nonparadoxical, because Liberace is out about his emulation of Rubinstein, the straight pianist, and closeted about his emulation of Horowitz, the gay one. Then again, he had already publicized the private Horowitz affair in "Playing Duets with the Masters"—and anyone with "Horowitz and Rubinstein on the brain," to cite the *New York Times*, would have known what that meant.

Fortunately, Liberace did measure up to one of the people he idolized, or should have said he idolized. He did know someone who did the same thing, and in the same way. Her name (her *single* name) is Hildegarde. Hildegarde was a swanky cocktail pianist who, like Liberace, hailed from Milwaukee and who made quite an impression when they appeared together at the Plaza in 1941—she being featured, he during intermissions. Liberace doesn't dwell upon the encounter, but his biographer does.

She swept into the room in a cloud of chiffon, her blond hair piled high on her head. Thunderous applause greeted her, and she sat down at the piano to play and sing "There'll Be Bluebirds Over the White Cliffs of Dover." The servicemen loved it, and she followed with "Praise the Lord and Pass the Ammunition." Then, she announced, it was time for something serious, and the room became silent as she played a Chopin nocturne followed by a Fritz Kreisler étude. She continued with a collection of songs she had made famous, finishing with "I'll Be Seeing You," which had servicemen and their dates crying. . . .

Walter marveled at how Hildegarde maintained total control of her audience. She called admirals and gobs, generals and GI's onto the floor and had the officers salute the enlisted men. If a drunken customer became noisy, she played and sang, "Show him the way to go home." When a baby cried out, it was "Rockabye baby, shut your little mouth." The audience roared in appreciation. They also did when she brushed off the piano lid and sang, "Dust a song at twilight."

Just as the audience assumed a festival mood, she silenced them with her climactic number, a Gershwin melody or her arrangement of Irving Berlin songs. At the last note, the spotlight blacked out, and for a brief, magical moment the room was silent. Then there was the onrush of cheers and applause. Hildegarde returned to bow deeply, but Walter noted that she never played an encore. "Always leave them wanting it to go on," she counseled him. (Thomas 32–33)

Liberace borrowed his humor, sentimentality, cozy manner, glamorous appearance, and middlebrow orientation from Hildegarde. He also borrowed her theme song. "I'll Be Seeing You" would soon become the aural equivalent of the Chopinesque candelabra. I'm sure he knew he borrowed them. I'd like to think he borrowed them because he knew he played as well as Hildegarde. I'd also like to think of this trouble-free, cross-sex cathexis as the key to Liberace's queer success—and as the not-so-secret secret of his (dare I say it?) self-satisfaction.

Coda

∾ I've been relearning two of the pieces I played in the memorial recitals—*Un Sospiro*, which I played for Linda, and the "Aeolian Harp" Etude, which I played for Steve. How do I sound these days? Not bad, for an amateur. And whom do I now hear? The concert étude reminds me of Liszt, Linda, and Louis Jourdan, who plays it in *Letter from an Unknown Woman*. The "Aeolian Harp" Etude reminds of Chopin, Liszt, my brother, my father—and, yes, Liberace, who sings it in *Sincerely Yours*.

REFERENCE MATTER

Notes

1. As Adorno says, "Nowhere is the struggle against the expert . . . more necessary than in music. For nowhere is the power of the dilettante greater. But expert and dilettante mutually complement each other. The dilettante feels he has been raised to a higher plane as soon as he understands the expert, whom he thereby elevates in his turn. The expert needs the dilettante in order to prove to himself that he isn't one. Together they form the twin poles of a middlebrow musical life whose hour has now struck" (*Quasi una Fantasia* 20).

2. See Copley 103.

3. It usually takes a (closet) antisentimentalist, just as it usually takes a (closet) elitist, to know another. As Sedgwick notes: "the attributive career of ['the sentimental' is] a vicariating one. For instance, it is well known that in Proust the snobbish characters are easy to recognize because they are the only ones who are able to recognize snobbism in others—hence, the only ones who really disapprove of it. Snobbism . . . can be discussed and attributed only by snobs, who are always right about it except in their own disclaimers of it. The same is true of the phenomenon of 'the sentimental'" (*Epistemology* 152).

4. According to Ignaz Paderewski, however, Cortot probably played a lot like Chopin; see Harasowski 190.

5. Gide's "colonization" of Chopin is typical, but retrograde. Whereas many nineteenth-century French authorities ignored Chopin's Polish nationality, few twentieth-century ones do; see Harasowski 120.

6. According to Barthes, pianos don't sing, even if instruments they accompany do: "the violin and the cello [in Schubert's first piano trio] 'sing' better—or, to be more exact, sing *more*—than the so-

prano or the baritone because, if there is a signification of sensuous phenomena, it is always in displacement, in substitution, i.e., ultimately, in *absence*, that it is most brilliantly manifest"("Romantic Song" 287).

7. Adorno thinks along more conventional lines: "[All] musical gesture [derives] from speech. When Beethoven calls for one of the bagatelles in Opus 33 to be played 'parlando,' he only makes explicit something that is a universal characteristic of music" (*Quasi una Fantasia* 1).

8. Adorno takes the unmistakable individuality for which Schumann praised Chopin as a sign of structural weakness. God forbid that he would ever have heard Gide play the A minor Prélude, an easier selection than the Barcarolle, but a "baffling miniature" of which—in a passage Lawrence Kramer describes as "helpless" and "solipsistic" (72)—Gide writes: "This is no concert piece. . . . But played in a whisper for oneself alone, its indefinable emotion cannot be exhausted, nor that kind of almost physical terror, as if one were before a world glimpsed in passing, of a world hostile to tenderness, from which human affection is excluded" (*Notes* 46).

9. According to Anthony Newcomb, Schumann deploys what "Romantic novelists called *Witz*—the faculty by which subtle underlying connections are discovered (or revealed) in a surface of apparent incoherence" (169).

CHAPTER 2

1. See Kalberg.

2. See Michalowski 295; Ostwald 115.

3. See Sedgwick, *Between Men*.

4. See Martin on the "sensuality" of piano playing: "When we play Beethoven's music, we are duplicating his *physical world* and *his very pianistic actions*, which allows us to enter his world in a way the nonperformer never can" (38).

5. See Korsyn, a Bloomian "inter-reading" of Brahms's Romanze, Op. 118, No. 5, and its "central precursor text," Chopin's Berceuse, Op. 57: "Brahms's coda negotiates the *apophrades* through what one might call a metaleptic reversal of [his] middle section, which was so closely modelled on the Berceuse" (18, 55–56).

6. Koestenbaum finds gay male stereotypes "obliquely inspiring, and a source of wonder" (*Queen's Throat* 58).

7. See Kopelson, "Wilde."

8. I'm using "bitch" in its literal sense; see Ackerley, *My Dog Tulip*.

9. In point of fact, Ackerley was an *amateur* homosexual who, like Gide, loathed fellatio: "It is a form of pleasure I myself have seldom enjoyed, passively or actively, preferring the kiss on the lips, nor have I ever been good at it. Some technical skill seems required and a re-traction of the teeth which, perhaps because mine are too large or unsuitably arranged, seem always to get in the way" (*My Father* 129–30).

10. See, e.g., Silverman.

11. "Whereas in the nineteenth century it was images of women in relation to domestic suffering and death that occupied the most po-tent, symptomatic, and, perhaps, friable or volatile place in the sen-timental *imaginaire* of middle-class culture, for the succeeding cen-tury . . . it has been images of agonistic male self-constitution" (Sedg-wick, *Epistemology* 147). See also Leppert, "Sexual Identity, Death, and the Family Piano in the Nineteenth Century," in *Sight of Sound*.

12. Derrida's citation ("limits of truth") is to Diderot's *Essai sur la vie de Sénèque le philosophe*.

CHAPTER 3

1. See Kincaid 312. See also Ariès, *Centuries of Childhood* 25, 29–30, 329, and "Thoughts on the History of Homosexuality" 67–68.

2. See Sedgwick, *Epistemology* 243.

3. One *New York Times* music critic, imagining noblemen like Beckford, described Thalberg as "a fox hunting squire of Merrie Eng-land" (quoted in Loesser 501).

4. See Loggins: "When the program ended, Chopin went back-stage, took Moreau by the hand, thanked him for choosing his con-certo, congratulated him on his interpretation, and prophesied that he would have great success as a virtuoso" (58). See also Gottschalk xxii.

5. See Bony 45, 189. The lithograph was published in Budapest in 1873 by István Halász to celebrate the fiftieth anniversary of Liszt's Vienna debut and is reproduced at the front of this book.

6. Ramann doesn't appear to have read the reviews, which weren't exactly glowing. For example, a Herr Kanne wrote in the *Wiener allgemeine musikalische Zeitung* (Apr. 26, 1823): "One has to allow this talented boy sufficient due; he played with fluency and elegance, although he lacked physical strength, a lack that one noticed particularly in the performance of the concerto."

7. See La Mara, *Briefwechsel* 116.

8. See Horowitz-Barnay. See also Frimmel.

9. As Keiler explains: "The original meaning of the *Weihekuss*, a paternal blessing of a son about to accept the challenge of manhood, is here turned into a recognition of accomplishment and participation in tradition" ("Liszt and Beethoven" 128).

10. Keiler isn't the first to find Horowitz-Barnay incredible; see Raabe 230 n. 12.

11. As Walker himself points out, Beethoven didn't move to the Schwarzpanier house until 1825 (*Liszt* 1: 84 n. 35).

12. Quoted in Walker, *Liszt* 1: 78.

CHAPTER 4

1. See Wexman 191, 199.

2. "He sat down and began to play . . . a wild Hungarian rhapsody by an unknown composer with a crack-jaw name" (Wilde, *Teleny* 25).

3. See Kopelson, "Wilde's Love-Deaths," in *Love's Litany*.

4. As Adorno puts it: "It sounds tremendously difficult and at all events loud. But it is comfortingly easy to play: the child knows that the colossal effect cannot misfire and that he is assured in advance of a triumph that has been achieved without effort. The Prelude preserves this triumph for infantile adults" (*Quasi una Fantasia* 38).

5. B. J. begins on bottom but ends on top, a *bouleversement* I attribute to Chuck's off-beat programming. If he'd played Satie, Debussy, and then Rachmaninov, B. J. would move from top to bottom.

6. Liszt, "Letter to Joseph d'Ortigue" (*Gazette musicale* [1839]), in *Artist's Journey* 164–65.

7. Jozef Elsner, the Director of the Warsaw Conservatory, had in fact been married. The film's false bachelorization underscores the homosociality of his attachment to Chopin. See Chopin, *Letters* 30.

8. In reality, of course, Chopin wasn't a concert pianist.

9. *Mazeppa*, based on a story that fascinated Byron as well, concerns a Ukrainian noblemen who, having been caught *in flagrante delicto* with another man's wife, is tied naked to a wild horse. The horse is driven into the night and finally collapses. Critics have remarked "that horses aren't the only animals to collapse under the strain of Mazeppa"; see Morrison 5.

10. This was, in fact, the case. Chopin, in a passage that suggests he cathected Liszt, once wrote: "Liszt is playing my études, and transporting me outside of my respectable thoughts. I should like to steal from him the way to play my own études" (*Letters* 171).

11. See, e.g., London *Times*, May 16, 1855: "Chopin was essentially a drawing-room composer. Away from his nocturnes and mazurkas, he became as trivial and incoherent as in those attractive trifles he was earnest and individual."

12. According to Richard Kaye, however, "Henry James would have written like Edith Wharton if he'd been a man" (personal communication).

13. According to Alfred Hipkins, of the Broadwood firm, Chopin "kept his elbows close to his sides and played only with finger touch—no weight from the arms" (Schonberg, *Great Pianists* 157). According to Charles Salaman, Thalberg never lost his tranquil ease of manner. The motionlessness, in and of itself, didn't feminize them. Ignaz Moscheles, for example, called Thalberg's bearing "soldier-like" (*Great Pianists* 184).

14. According to Hallé, Liszt "is in perpetual motion: now he stamps with his feet, now waves his arms in the air, now he does this, now that" (Schonberg, *Great Pianists* 166).

15. See Fétis, "Thalberg and Liszt" (*Gazette musicale* [Apr. 23, 1837]), in Liszt, *Artist's Journey* 26–27. See also Heine, "Confidential Letter" (*Gazette musicale* [Feb. 4, 1838]), in *Artist's Journey* 224.

16. Schumann had two musical alter egos: "Florestan," an extrovert, and "Eusebius," an introvert. Adjacent sections of *Carnaval*, for example, bear these names. I won't pay much attention to this division. For one thing, Schumann didn't perform and so wasn't read the way Chopin and Liszt were. He was read through Clara, who did perform—a fascinating topic that exceeds the scope of my analysis.

For another, Florestan and Eusebius have more to do with manic depression (Schumann's mental state) than with androgyny.

17. See Sedgwick, "The Beast in the Closet," in *Epistemology*.

18. See Kramer 22, 24, 30–31.

19. See Charles Rollinat, "Souvenir de Nohant," *Le Temps* (Sept. 1, 1874). Rollinat was the brother of a close friend of Sand.

20. These are undesirable characteristics, of course. According to Murray Perahia, for example, "One instinctively doesn't want to be thought of as a miniaturist [because the word is] pejorative" (Kimmelman).

21. Gould is the "Bobby Fischer of the piano," writes Schonberg. "Like the eccentric chess genius, he was an amazing talent who retired early and went into seclusion" (*Great Pianists* 477).

22. See Schonberg, *Horowitz* 131.

23. Some critics try but fail to *conflate* the two pianists. See, e.g., Taruskin: "Strange to say, many of the same critics who work hard to discredit Horowitz adulate Glenn Gould, an even loftier tamperer with texts. Why the double standard? Because Gould epitomizes monastic unworldliness and intellectual abstraction, whereas Horowitz was urbane and visceral. Even more to the point, Gould upgraded modernist disregard of the audience to the point of anhedonia, while Horowitz aimed to please. All of which is to say that of the two, Gould was by far the truer Romantic."

24. "I like . . . Glenn Gould," Barthes writes; "I don't like Arthur Rubinstein" (*Roland Barthes* 116–17).

25. See Sedgwick, "Proust and the Spectacle of the Closet," in *Epistemology*.

26. Francois Girard's *32 Short Films About Glenn Gould* (1994) provides a similar pleasure: a ludicrous self-interview in which Gould denies his homosexuality.

27. As Dubal reports: "The piano [was] his sexual organ, the audience, his lover. I once asked him what he thought of when playing Scriabin's Fifth Sonata for an audience. He loudly responded, 'I want to *fock* them'" (*Evenings* 16).

28. The bad reviews Horowitz received for this Carnegie Hall performance led to his second retirement (Schonberg, *Horowitz* 174). Schonberg still finds the Schnabel Schubert ("overpowering authority and a masculine sense of poetry") far less episodic than the Ho-

rowitz ("more feminine, more interesting harmonically"; *Horowitz* 352).

29. See Schonberg, *Horowitz* 166–67.

30. See Schonberg, *Horowitz* 240. Pogorelich is an *enfant terrible* as well (Mach 2: 248).

31. See, e.g., Hadow: "For the larger types of art, for the broad architectonic laws of structure on which they are based, [Chopin] exhibited an almost total disregard. His works in Sonata form and in the forms cognate to the Sonata, are with no exception, the failure of a genius that has altogether overstepped his bounds. . . . In structure, he is a child, playing with a few simple types and almost helpless as soon as he advances beyond them" (151, 168).

32. Clara Schumann considered the Liszt Sonata "gruesome": "just empty noise, not a single wholesome idea, everything in confusion, impossible to find any clear harmonic sequence in it" (Litzmann 2: 317). Eduard Hanslick, a contemporary critic, concurred: "I have never come across a more refined, more impudent concatenation of the most disparate elements—or such empty raving, such a bloody struggle against everything musical" (Hanslick 318). Karl Klindworth liked it, though.

33. Although a number of virtuosos (Ferruccio Busoni, Eugen d'Albert, Arthur Friedheim) played the Liszt Sonata, it didn't enter the repertoire until Horowitz recorded it in 1932. See Dubal, *Evenings* 298.

34. Apart from an original cast album of *Damn Yankees*, broken in half by my sister after I'd played "Whatever Lola Wants" one too many times, the first record I cathected was an old 78 rpm of the Horowitz Tchaikovsky. Not knowing better, however, I played the sides at random and so came to know both the Concerto and the performer as abnormally fractured.

35. See Schonberg: "Rubinstein always claimed that he had been a sloppy pianist before he married; that not until then did he buckle down and really practice"(*Horowitz* 187).

CHAPTER 5

1. See Trinh: "In writing close to the other of the other, I can only choose to maintain a self-reflexively critical relationship toward the

material, a relationship that defines both the subject written and the writing subject, undoing the I while asking 'what do I want wanting to *know* you or me?'" (76).

2. These remarks are fictitious. Jeffrey Swann doesn't really defame pianists associated with the Van Cliburn Competition.

3. The references are to John Schlesinger's film *Madame Sousatzka* (1988).

4. These figures can be found in Daly's *Wickedary*.

5. As Wilde says: "Do you wish to love? Use Love's Litany, and the words will create the yearning from which the world fancies that they spring" ("The Critic as Artist" 399).

6. "I don't know whether I like you or not," Edna tells Mademoiselle Reisz at their first tête-à-tête. It's a remark the teacher finds "pleasing" (Chopin, *Awakening* 526).

CHAPTER 6

1. See Drewal 149.

2. Liberace audiences do, in fact, *see* the music; "Liberace appeared with a piano inlaid with etched mirrors, a white cape, and a pale blue, sequined tuxedo. He paid tribute to Chopin, his 'favorite' composer. Steam was pumped in to cover the floor of the stage; the colored dancing waters spouted to the rhythms of the music on a second level; and behind that another elevator rose carrying dancer Lewis, who had his partner, Kuniko, in a high lift. . . . The dancing waters continued, a combination of green, red, yellow, blue, orange, changing to blue and green, with concomitant changes in rhythms and textures. Liberace's piano began to turn, to thunderous applause from the audience. . . . At the finish, Liberace . . . told the audience he was 'so glad' they enjoyed listening to the music of Chopin: the visual sensory stimuli in fact diverted attention from Chopin" (Drewal 157–58).

3. See Raykoff.

4. Using Barthesian terms, Garber argues that unmarked transvestism is "received" but not "read" (356). Liberace never "read" himself as a cross-dresser and considered his stage attire "one step short of drag" (Thomas 215). Some audience members, however, did read him as one. "Quite frankly," groused Las Vegas *Sun* critic Dick Maurice, "[he looks] like a female impersonator auditioning for 'An Evening at La Cage'" (Thomas 254).

5. Liberace himself didn't credit the ideology that informs *Letter from an Unknown Woman*. "Fucking," he reasoned, "[doesn't] sap your creative energy" (Thomas 234).

6. See Meyer.

7. According to Bergman, the effect, which works not by dismantling the gender system but by trading on its blindness, "is hardly a foolproof strategy: Oscar Wilde's deployment of it in his trials failed miserably" (14).

8. Wakoski, "Why My Mother Likes Liberace"; copyright © 1986 by Diane Wakoski; reprinted from *Emerald Ice: Selected Poems, 1962–1987* with the permission of Black Sparrow Press.

9. "Sodomy" used to denote other deviant behaviors as well as anal intercourse, including treason and witchcraft—making the term "fag hag" rather redundant. As Bredbeck notes: "During the period in question, 'sodomy' meant sodomy. But it also meant bestiality, lesbianism, heterosexual anal intercourse, adultery, minority and alien status, heresy, political insurgence, witchcraft and sorcery, ad infinitum" (xi–xii).

10. Garber, however, reads Liberace's flying act as an extraordinary instance of "marked" transvestism. "Already 'ageless,' a parodic version of the eternal 'boy,' with his face-lifts, hairpieces, and increasingly heavy makeup, he conceived of a desire to become (although he never says so): Peter Pan. Ostensibly this fantasy was triggered by the aerodynamic effect of his cape as he left the stage one night; soon he had enlisted Peter Foy, of the English Flying Foys, the man who had taught two generations of female Peter Pans, including Mary Martin, to 'fly.' Liberace here is, for a moment, a triumph of metonymic transvestism, a middle-aged man imitating a woman who plays a fantasy changeling boy" (359).

11. *The Loved One* is based on the novel by Evelyn Waugh, but the Liberace role was created by the screenwriters (Terry Southern and Christopher Isherwood). Liberace himself considered the part "prissy" (*Autobiography* 109).

12. One man, wearing a diamond ring, a diamond earring, and several gold necklaces, said he "loved that man" and wished he "could be like him" (Reinhold).

13. As Garber remarks: "[By the time] Elvis returned to Las Vegas, heavier, in pancake makeup, wearing a white jumpsuit with an

elaborate jeweled belt and cape, crooning pop songs to a microphone . . . he had become Liberace. Even his fans were now middle-aged matrons and blue-haired grandmothers, who praised him as a good son who loved his mother" (364).

14. Liberace believed the two of them represented the real thing: "An audience can spot a phony. Whether it's a classical, pop, or rock concert, people love sincerity and integrity. There have been performers who've been disappointing to me because I felt they were just going to take the money and run. And then there are others—like Jennifer Holliday, who almost literally sings her guts out. How can you not be moved by the intensity of feeling you get from that kind of performer? There aren't many around capable of giving an audience that charge. Judy Garland was one, Elvis Presley another" (*Wonderful Private World* 144).

15. See Sedgwick, "White Glasses" 193–208.

16. See Sontag 282. For an introduction to Florence Foster Jenkins, see Groover.

17. See Radway.

18. See Yingling: "If gay men often seem overly enamored of the very culture that stigmatizes them (the collector or connoisseur who gives proof of his possession and appreciation of 'class' and his refined values of exchange in his every acquisition and act—the stereotype Liberace played on; the gay bureaucrat who, like the title character in *The Dresser*, serves his master patiently and in suffering love; Oscar Wilde via Dorian Gray): we must see beneath this the paradox that such men actually exist without a culture, without reference outside themselves" (33–34).

19. See Sedgwick, "Proust and the Spectacle of the Closet," in *Epistemology*.

20. The lyrics are by Jon Arterton, a member of this openly gay group (*The Flirtations Live: Out on the Road* [Flirt Records FL 1001]).

21. See Butler 137 ("In imitating gender, drag implicitly reveals the imitative structure of gender itself—as well as its contingency") and Hansen 25 ("The more desperately Valentino himself emphasized attributes of physical prowess and virility, the more perfectly he played the part of the male impersonator, brilliant counterpart to the female 'female' impersonators of the American screen such as Mae

West or the vamps of his own films"). See also Castle; Moon and Sedgwick; Robertson.

22. See Smart.

23. See Thomas 13.

24. "With the greatest conceit in the world, I reasoned that if my idol, Paderewski, could become world famous using only his last name, Liberace couldn't be so bad" (*Autobiography* 81).

25. "I was brazenly placing myself in the same league as these great names of music [and] realized that in doing so I had to be very good" (*Autobiography* 84).

26. See Schonberg: "Paderewski became the most popular and highest paid pianist in history up to that time, and the mystery to his colleagues was how he did it. He was not a great technician or a great musician in their estimation" (*Virtuosi* 216).

Works Cited

Ackerley, J. R. *My Dog Tulip*. 1965. Reprint, New York: Poseidon, 1987.

————. *My Father and Myself*. New York: Coward-McCann, 1969.

Adorno, Theodor W. *Mahler: A Musical Physiognomy*. Trans. Edmund Jephcott. Chicago: University of Chicago Press, 1992.

————. *Quasi una Fantasia: Essays on Modern Music*. Trans. Rodney Livingstone. London: Verso, 1992.

Ariès, Philippe. *Centuries of Childhood: A Social History of Family Life*. Trans. Robert Baldick. New York: Knopf, 1962.

————. "Thoughts on the History of Homosexuality." In Philippe Ariès and André Bejin, eds., *Western Sexuality: Practice and Precept in Past and Present Times*. Trans. Anthony Forster. Oxford: Basil Blackwell, 1985.

Balzac, Honoré de. "Sarassine." In Roland Barthes, *S/Z*. Trans. Richard Miller. New York: Hill & Wang, 1974.

Barthes, Roland. *Camera Lucida: Reflections on Photography*. Trans. Richard Howard. New York: Hill & Wang, 1991.

————. *The Grain of the Voice: Interviews 1962–1980*. Trans. Linda Coverdale. New York: Hill & Wang, 1985.

————. "The Grain of the Voice." In *The Responsibility of Forms*. Trans. Richard Howard. New York: Hill & Wang, 1985.

————. "Inaugural Lecture, Collège de France." Trans. Richard Miller. In *A Barthes Reader*. Ed. Susan Sontag. New York: Hill & Wang, 1982.

————. *Incidents*. Trans. Richard Howard. Berkeley: University of California Press, 1992.

————. "Listening." In *The Responsibility of Forms*. Trans. Richard Howard. New York: Hill & Wang, 1985.

————. *A Lover's Discourse: Fragments*. Trans. Richard Howard. New York: Hill & Wang, 1978.

———. "Loving Schumann." In *The Responsibility of Forms*. Trans. Richard Howard. New York: Hill & Wang, 1985.

———. "Musica Practica." In *The Responsibility of Forms*. Trans. Richard Howard. New York: Hill & Wang, 1985.

———. "Rasch." In *The Responsibility of Forms*. Trans. Richard Howard. New York: Hill & Wang, 1985.

———. *Roland Barthes by Roland Barthes*. Trans. Richard Howard. New York: Hill & Wang, 1977.

———. "The Romantic Song." In *The Responsibility of Forms*. Trans. Richard Howard. New York: Hill & Wang, 1985.

———. *S/Z*. Trans. Richard Miller. New York: Hill & Wang, 1974.

Bergman, David, ed. *Camp Grounds: Style and Homosexuality*. Amherst: University of Massachusetts Press, 1993.

Berlioz, Hector. "Liszt." *Gazette musicale* (June 12, 1836): 198–200.

Bersani, Leo. "Is the Rectum a Grave?" *October* 43 (Winter 1987): 197–222.

Bloom, Harold. *The Anxiety of Influence: A Theory of Poetry*. London: Oxford University Press, 1973.

Bony, Robert. *La Vie de Franz Liszt par l'image*. Geneva, 1936.

Bredbeck, Gregory W. *Sodomy and Interpretation: Marlowe to Milton*. Ithaca, N.Y.: Cornell University Press, 1991.

Butler, Judith. *Gender Trouble: Feminism and the Subversion of Identity*. New York: Routledge, 1990.

Castle, Terry. "In Praise of Brigitte Fassbaender: Reflections on Diva Worship." In Corrine E. Blackmer and Patricia Juliana Smith, eds., *En Travesti: Women, Gender Subversion, Opera*. New York: Columbia University Press, 1995.

Chopin, Frédéric. *Chopin's Letters*. Trans. E. L. Voynich. New York: Dover, 1988.

Chopin, Kate. *The Awakening*. In Donald Kesey, ed., *Contexts for Criticism*. Mountain View, Calif.: Mayfield, 1994.

Copley, Antony. *Sexual Moralities in France, 1780–1980: New Ideas on the Family, Divorce and Homosexuality*. London: Routledge, 1989.

Corder, Frederick. *Ferencz (François) Liszt*. New York: Harper, 1925.

Crutchfield, Will. "The Man Who Would Be Liszt." *New York Times*, Feb. 14, 1993, pp. 25–27.

Daly, Mary. *Websters' First Intergalactic Wickedary of the English Language*. New York: HarperCollins, 1987.

Derrida, Jacques. *Aporias*. Trans. Thomas Dutoit. Stanford, Calif.: Stanford University Press, 1993.

———. *The Post Card: From Socrates to Freud and Beyond*. Trans. Alan Bass. Chicago: University of Chicago Press, 1987.

Dostoevsky, Fyodor. *The Possessed*. Trans. Andrew R. MacAndrew. New York: Penguin, 1962.

Drewal, Margaret Thompson. "The Camp Trace in Corporate America: Liberace and the Rockettes at Radio City Music Hall." In Moe Meyer, ed., *The Politics and Poetics of Camp*. New York: Routledge, 1994.

Dubal, David. *Evenings with Horowitz: A Personal Portrait*. New York: Birch Lane, 1991.

———. *Reflections from the Keyboard: The World of the Concert Pianist*. New York: Summit, 1984.

Fay, Amy. *Music-Study in Germany: The Classic Memoir of the Romantic Era*. 1880. Reprint, New York: Dover, 1965.

Frimmel, Theodor von. *Beethoven Studien II. Bausteine zu einer Lebensgeschichte des Meisters*. Munich, 1906.

Garber, Marjorie. *Vested Interests: Cross-Dressing and Cultural Anxiety*. New York: HarperCollins, 1993.

Gay, Peter. *The Bourgeois Experience: Victoria to Freud*. Vol. 2, *The Tender Passion*. London: Oxford University Press, 1986.

Gide, André. *The Immoralist*. Trans. Richard Howard. New York: Knopf, 1970.

———. *The Journals of André Gide*, 4 vols. Trans. Justin O'Brien. New York: Knopf, 1947–51.

———. *Notes on Chopin*. Trans. Bernard Frechtman. New York: Philosophical Library, 1949.

———. *Oeuvres complètes*. Paris: Gallimard, 1932.

———. *Si le grain ne meurt*. Paris: Gallimard, 1955.

———. *Straight Is the Gate*. Trans. Dorothy Bussy. New York: Knopf, 1949.

Gottschalk, Louis Moreau. *Notes of a Pianist*. Ed. Jeanne Behrend. New York: Knopf, 1964.

Gould, Glenn. "Streisand as Schwarzkopf." Review of *Classical Barbra* (Columbia M33452). *Hi Fidelity*, May 1976, pp. 73–75.

Groover, David L. *Skeletons from the Opera Closet*. New York: St. Martin's, 1986.

Hadow, W. H. *Studies in Modern Music.* New York: Macmillan, 1893.

Hamburger, Klara. *Liszt.* Trans. Gulya Gulyás. Trans. revised Paul Merrick. Budapest: Kossuth, 1987.

Hanslick, Eduard. *Concerte, Componisten, und Virtuosen der letzten fünfzehn Jahre, 1870–1885.* Berlin: Allgemeiner Verein für Deutsche Literatur, 1896.

Hansen, Miriam. "Pleasure, Ambivalence, Identification: Valentino and Female Spectatorship." *Cinema Journal* 25, no. 4 (Summer 1986): 6–32.

Hanson, Ellis. "Undead." In Diana Fuss, ed., *Inside/Out: Lesbian Theories, Gay Theories.* New York: Routledge, 1991.

Harasowski, Adam. *The Skein of Legends Around Chopin.* Glasgow: William MacLellan, 1967.

Hernández, Felisberto. "The Stray Horse." In *Piano Stories.* Trans. Luis Harss. New York: Marsilio, 1993.

Holland, Bernard. "In the Music World, Dead Men Have More Sales." *New York Times,* Oct. 29, 1992, p. B5.

Horowitz, Joseph. *The Ivory Trade: Piano Competitions and the Business of Music.* Boston: Northeastern University Press, 1990.

Horowitz-Barnay, Ilka. "Im Hause Franz Liszt." *Deutsche Revue* 22 (1898): 76–84.

Huneker, James. *Chopin: The Man and His Music.* New York: Dover, 1966.

Isherwood, Christopher. "On Ruegen Island (Summer 1931)." In *The Berlin Stories.* 1935. Reprint, New York: New Directions, 1963.

Janin, Jules. Untitled. *Journal des débats politiques et littéraires,* Apr. 3, 1837, p. 2.

Kalberg, Jeffrey. "The Harmony of the Tea Table: Gender and Ideology in the Piano Nocturne." *Representations* 39 (Summer 1992): 102–33.

Keiler, Allan. "Liszt and Beethoven: The Creation of a Personal Myth." *Nineteenth-Century Music* 12, no. 2 (Fall 1988): 116–31.

———. "Liszt Research and Walker's Liszt." *The Musical Quarterly* 10, no. 3 (Summer 1984): 374–403.

Kimmelman, Michael. "With Plenty of Time to Think, a Pianist Redirects his Career." *New York Times,* Apr. 3, 1994, p. H25.

Kincaid, James R. *Child-Loving: The Erotic Child and Victorian Culture.* New York: Routledge, 1992.

Koestenbaum, Wayne. "The Answer Is in the Garden." In *Ode to Anna Moffo and Other Poems*. New York: Persea, 1990.

———. "Piano Life." In *Rhapsodies of a Repeat Offender*. New York: Persea, 1994.

———. *The Queen's Throat: Opera, Homosexuality, and the Mystery of Desire*. New York: Poseidon, 1993.

Kopelson, Kevin. *Love's Litany: The Writing of Modern Homoerotics*. Stanford, Calif.: Stanford University Press, 1994.

———. "Wilde, Barthes, and the Orgasmics of Truth." *Genders* 7 (Spring 1990): 22–31.

Korsyn, Kevin. "Towards a New Poetics of Musical Influence." *Music Analysis* 10, no. 1–2 (1991): 3–72.

Kramer, Lawrence. *Music as Cultural Practice, 1800–1900*. Berkeley: University of California Press, 1990.

Kristeva, Julia. *Powers of Horror: An Essay on Abjection*. Trans. Leon S. Roudiez. New York: Columbia University Press, 1982.

———. *Tales of Love*. Trans. Leon S. Roudiez. New York: Columbia University Press, 1987.

Kuerti, Anton. "All That Glitters Is Not Gould." *Toronto Globe and Mail*, Feb. 12, 1994, p. C9.

Leppert, Richard. *The Sight of Sound: Music, Representation, and the History of the Body*. Berkeley: University of California Press, 1993.

Liberace. *Liberace: An Autobiography*. New York: Putnam's, 1973.

———. *The Wonderful Private World of Liberace*. New York: Harper & Row, 1986.

Liberace in Las Vegas. Warner Home Video: Pacific Newport Enterprises, Inc., 1980.

Limmer, Ruth. *Journey Around My Room: The Autobiography of Louise Bogan*. New York: Penguin, 1981.

Liszt, Franz. *An Artist's Journey: Lettres d'un bachelier ès musique, 1835–1841*. Trans. Charles Suttori. Chicago: University of Chicago Press, 1989.

Litzmann, Berthold. *Clara Schumann: Ein Künstlerleben nach Tagebüchern und Briefen*, 3 vols. Leipzig: Druck und Verlag von Breitkopf & Härtel, 1925.

Loesser, Arthur. *Men, Women, and Pianos: A Social History*. New York: Simon and Schuster, 1954.

Loggins, Vernon. *Where the World Ends: The Life of Louis Moreau Gottschalk*. Baton Rouge: Louisiana State University Press, 1958.

Mach, Elyse. *Great Contemporary Pianists Speak for Themselves*, 2 vols. New York: Dover, 1991.

MacKail, Clare. "Early Days." In Howard Ferguson, ed., *Myra Hess by Her Friends*. London: Hamish Hamilton, 1966.

Mann, Thomas. "Das Wunderkind." In Mann, *Die Erzählungen*. Oldenburgh: Fischer, 1966.

La Mara [Marie Lipsius], ed. *Briefwechsel zwischen Franz Liszt und Carl Alexander, Grossherzog von Sachsen*. Leipzig, 1909.

———. *Liszt und die Frauen*. Leipzig, 1911.

Martin, James L. "Beethoven and the Purpose of Difficulty." *The Piano Quarterly* 154 (Summer 1991): 37–42.

Métayer, Bernard. "Gide et Chopin." *Bulletin des Amis d'André Gide* 18, no. 85 (1990): 65–91.

Meyer, Richard. "Rock Hudson's Body." In Diana Fuss, ed., *Inside/Out: Lesbian Theories, Gay Theories*. New York: Routledge, 1991.

Michalowski, K. "Frederic Chopin." In S. Sadie, ed., *The New Grove Dictionary of Music and Musicians*, vol. 4. London: MacMillan, 1980.

Moon, Michael, and Eve Kosofsky Sedgwick. "Divinity: A Dossier, A Performance Piece, A Little-Understood Emotion." *Discourse* 13, no. 1 (Fall–Winter 1990–91): 12–39.

Morrison, Bryce. "Liszt: Transcendental Studies, S139." Liner notes to Jorge Bolet, *Liszt: Etudes d'exécution transcendante s. 139* (London 414 601-2).

Neal, Harry Lee. *Wave as You Pass*. Philadelphia: Lippincott, 1958.

Newcomb, Anthony. "Schumann and Late Eighteenth-Century Narrative Strategies." *Nineteenth-Century Music* 11 (1987): 164–74.

Ostwald, Peter. *Schumann: The Inner Voices of a Musical Genius*. Boston: Northeastern University Press, 1985.

Perényi, Eleanor. *Liszt: The Artist as Romantic Hero*. Boston: Atlantic Monthly / Little, Brown, 1974.

Plantinga, Leon. *Clementi: His Life and Music*. London: Oxford University Press, 1977.

Proust, Marcel. *Remembrance of Things Past*, 3 vols. Trans. C. K. Scott Moncrieff and Terence Kilmartin. New York: Random, 1981.

Raabe, Peter. *Franz Liszt: Leben und Schaffen*, vol. 1. Stuttgart, 1931.

Radway, Janice. "Mail-Order Culture and Its Critics: The Book-of-the-Month Club, Commodification and Consumption, and the Problem of Cultural Authority." In Lawrence Grossberg, Cary Nelson, and Paula Treichler, eds., *Cultural Studies*. New York: Routledge, 1992.

Ramann, Lina. *Franz Liszt: Artist and Man, 1911–1840*, vol. 1. Trans. E. Cowdery. London: W. H. Allen, 1882.

Raykoff, Ivan. "Transcription and Transgression: The Camp Pianist from Liszt to Liberace." Paper presented at the Sixth North American Conference on Lesbian, Gay, and Bisexual Studies ("InQueery/InTheory/InDeed"), Iowa City, Iowa, Nov. 17–20, 1994.

Reinhold, Robert. "Liberace Auction: Glittering Ghost." *New York Times*, Aug. 28, 1987, p. C24.

Rezits, Joseph. "The Teaching of Isabelle Vengerova." *Piano Quarterly* 106 (Summer 1979): 16–23.

Rivette, Jacques, and François Truffaut. "Interview with Max Ophuls." Trans. Jennifer Batchelor. In Paul Willemen, ed., *Ophuls*. London: British Film Institute, 1978.

Robertson, Pamela. "'The Kinda Comedy that Imitates Me': Mae West's Identification with the Feminist Camp." In David Bergman, ed., *Camp Grounds: Style and Homosexuality*. Amherst: University of Massachusetts Press, 1993.

Rollinat, Charles. "Souvenir de Nohant." *Le Temps*, Sept. 1, 1874.

Rubinstein, Arthur. *My Many Years*. New York: Knopf, 1980.

Said, Edward. *Musical Elaborations*. New York: Columbia University Press, 1991.

Salaman, Charles. "Pianists of the Past." *Blackwood's Magazine*, Sept. 1901, pp. 307–30.

Schindler, Anton F. *Biographie von Ludwig van Beethoven*. Münster, 1840; enlarged 1845; rev. 1860.

Schonberg, Harold C. *The Great Pianists: From Mozart to the Present*. New York: Simon & Schuster, 1987.

———. *Horowitz: His Life and Music*. New York: Simon & Schuster, 1992.

———. *The Virtuosi: Classical Music's Legendary Performers from Paganini to Pavarotti*. New York: Random House, 1988.

Schumann, Robert. *Carnaval*, Op. 9. In Max Vogrich, ed., *Schirmer's Library of Musical Classics*, vol. 89. New York: G. Schirmer, 1893.

————. *Schumann on Music: A Selection from the Writings*. Trans. and ed. Henry Pleasants. New York: Dover, 1988.

Sedgwick, Eve Kosofsky. *Between Men: English Literature and Male Homosocial Desire*. New York: Columbia University Press, 1985.

————. *Epistemology of the Closet*. Berkeley: University of California Press, 1990.

————. "White Glasses." *The Yale Journal of Criticism* 5, no.3 (Fall 1992): 193–208.

Silverman, Kaja. *Male Subjectivity at the Margins*. New York: Routledge, 1992.

Slonimsky, Nicolas. "'Musique': Reminiscences of a Vanished World and a Great Teacher." *The Piano Teacher*, Sept.–Oct. 1963, pp. 2–4.

Smalley, Stuart [Al Franken]. *I'm Good Enough, I'm Smart Enough, and Doggone It, People Like Me!* New York: Dell, 1992.

Smart, Mary Ann. "The Lost Voice of Rosine Stoltz." In Corrine E. Blackmer and Patricia Juliana Smith, eds., *En Travesti: Women, Gender Subversion, Opera*. New York: Columbia University Press, 1995.

Sontag, Susan. "Notes on Camp." In *Against Interpretation and Other Essays*. New York: Dell, 1966.

Steiner, George. "Glenn Gould's Notes." *The New Yorker*, Nov. 23, 1992, pp. 137–41.

Stendhal. *Love*. Trans. Gilbert and Suzanne Sale. Harmondsworth: Penguin, 1975.

Stevens, Wallace. "Thirteen Ways of Looking at a Blackbird." In *The Palm at the End of the Mind*. Ed. Holly Stevens. New York: Vintage, 1972.

Taruskin, Richard. "Why Do They All Hate Horowitz?" *New York Times*, Nov. 28, 1993, p. H31.

Taylor, Ronald. *Franz Liszt: The Man and His Music*. London: Grafton, 1986.

Thomas, Bob. *Liberace: The True Story*. New York: St. Martin's, 1987.

Thompson, Michael. *Rubbish Theory: The Creation and Destruction of Value*. Oxford: Oxford University Press, 1979.

Trinh T. Minh-ha. *Woman, Native, Other: Writing Postcoloniality and Feminism*. Bloomington: Indiana University Press, 1989.

Wakoski, Diane. "The Beautiful *Amanita Muscaria*." In *Why My Mother Likes Liberace: A Musical Selection.* Tucson: SUN/gemini, 1985.

———. "Virtuoso Literature for Two and Four Hands." In *Why My Mother Likes Liberace: A Musical Selection.* Tucson: SUN/gemini, 1985.

———. "Why My Mother Likes Liberace." In *Emerald Ice: Selected Poems 1962–1987.* Santa Rosa, Calif.: Black Sparrow Press, 1988.

Wald-Lasowski, Roman. "Ecriture et piano: Gide, Barthes, Chopin." In Raphael Célis, ed., *Littérature et musique.* Brussels: Facultés universitaires Saint-Louis, 1982.

Walker, Alan. *Franz Liszt.* Vol. 1, *The Virtuoso Years 1811–1847.* New York: Knopf, 1983.

———. *Franz Liszt.* Vol. 2, *The Weimar Years 1848–1861.* New York: Knopf, 1989.

———. "Liszt's Musical Background." In Alan Walker, ed., *Franz Liszt: The Man and His Music.* London: Barrie & Jenkins, 1970.

Welty, Eudora. "June Recital." In *The Golden Apples.* 1949. Reprint, New York: Harcourt Brace Jovanovich, 1977.

Wexman, Virginia Wright, ed. *Letter from an Unknown Woman.* New Brunswick, N.J.: Rutgers University Press, 1986.

Wilde, Oscar. "The Critic as Artist." In *The Artist as Critic: Critical Writings of Oscar Wilde.* Ed. Richard Ellmann. Chicago: University of Chicago Press, 1968.

———. *The Importance of Being Earnest.* In *The Complete Illustrated Stories, Plays, and Poems of Oscar Wilde.* London: Chancellor, 1986.

———. *Teleny.* 1893. Reprint, San Francisco: Gay Sunshine, 1984.

Woolf, Virginia. *Jacob's Room.* New York: Harcourt Brace Jovanovich, 1978.

———. *The Waves.* New York: Harcourt Brace Jovanovich, 1978.

Yingling, Thomas E. *Hart Crane and the Homosexual Text.* Chicago: University of Chicago Press, 1990.

Index

In this index "f" after a number indicates a separate reference on the next page, and "ff" indicates separate references on the next two pages. A continuous discussion over two or more pages is indicated by a span of numbers. *Passim* is used for a cluster of references in close but not consecutive sequence.

Abjection, 52, 54, 132, 146, 154
Ackerley, J. R., 49–50, 73, 173n9
Adolescence, 61–62, 71, 75f, 78–79, 122
Adorno, Theodor, 10, 33, 37, 48, 58, 90f, 107, 171n11, 172n7, 172n8, 174n4
d'Agoult, Marie, 72, 94f
AIDS, 37, 43, 55, 139, 153
Albéniz, Isaac, 15
d'Albert, Eugen, 177n33
Althusser, Louis, 118
Amateurism, 7–33, 40f, 88, 90, 98, 108, 117, 119, 156, 167, 173n9, 174n4
Andrews, Julie, 42, 45, 54
Androgyny, 42, 44, 98, 175n16
Argerich, Martha, 117
Arrau, Claudio, 14, 106

Bach, Johann Sebastian, 24, 31, 70
Balzac, Honoré de, 111, 133–34
Barthes, Roland, 7–33 *passim*, 46–48, 53, 57f, 73, 75, 95, 105, 109, 118, 129–30, 133–35, 151–56 *passim*, 178n4; *Camera Lucida*, 46–48; "The Grain of the Voice," 15–20 *passim*; "Inaugural Lecture," 126; *Incidents*, 9; "Listening," 29; *A Lover's Discourse: Fragments*, 57, 77; "Loving Schumann," 16, 22, 32; "Musica Practica," 17, 28; "Rasch,"

17f, 22, 29f, 32, 149; *Roland Barthes by Roland Barthes*, 12, 19–20, 22ff, 30, 130; "The Romantic Song," 25f, 171n6; *S/Z*, 124, 133–34
Beckford, Peter, 63–65
Beckford, William, 63
Beethoven, Ludwig van, 27f, 31, 48, 51, 64, 67–77 *passim*, 85, 97, 100, 155, 163, 172n4; Bagatelles, 29, 172n7; "Hammerklavier" Sonata, 100; "Moonlight" Sonata, 10–11, 149; Piano Concerto No. 1, 70
Belgiojoso, Cristina, 100–102
Bergman, David, 143
Berlioz, Hector, 100
Bernstein, Leonard, 85, 128
Bersani, Leo, 23
Bloom, Harold, 46, 172n5
Blumenfeld, Felix, 107
Bogan, Louise, 124–26
Bösendorfer, 4, 12
Brahms, Johannes, 47f, 53, 85, 172n5
Bredbeck, Gregory, 179n9
Brendel, Alfred, 27
Bristol, Claude, 157
Bülow, Hans von, 18
Busoni, Ferruccio, 177n33
Butler, Judith, 155f, 180n21
Byron, George Gordon, 18, 111, 175n9

Camp, 14, 119, 120–21, 139, 148f,
  153–54, 162
Carnegie Hall, 1, 59, 149, 163, 176n28
Cassandra (William Neil Connor),
  151–52
Castration, 40, 86, 88, 94f, 120–21, 133
Cathexis, *see* Desirous identification
Child prodigies, 59–79, 126–27,
  132–33
Chopin, Frédéric, 8, 10–33 *passim*,
  37–58 *passim*, 66–67, 74, 85, 93,
  102, 105–11 *passim*, 120, 134f,
  139–46 *passim*, 150–55 *passim*,
  159ff, 165, 167, 171n4, 171n5, 173n4,
  178n2; vs. Liszt, 93–100 *passim*, 108
———, works of: "Aeolian Harp"
  Etude, 35, 50f, 95, 150, 167; Ballade
  in G minor, 15, 41, 95; Barcarolle,
  8, 26f, 31, 113, 172n8; Berceuse, 94,
  172n5; Fantasie-Impromptu, 95,
  134; "Funeral March" Sonata, 108;
  Mazurkas, 175n11; "Minute"
  Waltz, 149; Nocturnes, 39, 94, 164,
  175n11; Piano Concerto No. 1, 66;
  Polonaise in A-flat major, 37, 47,
  61f, 93ff, 161; Préludes, 18, 23,
  172n8; Sonata in B minor, 108
Chopin, Kate, 134–36, 150
Class, 11–13 *passim*, 20, 65–69 *passim*,
  85, 108, 118–19, 130–60 *passim*,
  180n18
Clementi, Muzio, 62–64, 79, 83, 97,
  107, 113
Cliburn, Van, 14, 109–10, 112f, 120–21
Closet, 13ff, 30, 55, 74, 103ff, 113, 148,
  152–53, 158, 171n3
Cole, Buddy (Scott Thompson), 159
Command Performance (porn
  video), 90–91
Corder, Frederick, 68
Cortot, Alfred, 22, 31, 171n4
Coward, Noel, 152–53
Crawford, Joan, 84
Crutchfield, Will, 103
Cultural capital, 11, 66, 87, 93, 110,
  118–19, 142f, 147–55 *passim*, 163f,
  180n18
Czerny, Carl, 64, 69f

Daly, Mary, 118, 127–28, 143
Dark Victory (film), 84
Dasein, 22, 35, 46, 51
Davis, Bette, 84, 127
Debussy, Claude, 91, 154, 174n5
De Groote, Steven, *see* Groote,
  Steven De
Derrida, Jacques, 54–58 *passim*, 79,
  99, 173n12
Desirous identification, 38–45
  passim, 48–54 *passim*, 65f, 73, 76,
  84–93 *passim*, 132, 157, 161, 165,
  172n5, 175n10, 177n34, 179n12
Development, 10, 32, 71, 146, 149
Dichter, Misha, 85, 88f
Diderot, Denis, 173n12
Diller, Phyllis, 157f
Divine (Glenn Milstead), 155
Doehler, Theodore, 64
Dostoevsky, Fyodor, 52
Drewal, Margaret, 143, 154–56 *passim*
Dubal, David, 106, 176n27
Duchin, Eddy, 162
The Dying Swan (film), 83f, 89

Egorov, Youri, 37, 55–56, 120
Elsner, Jozef, 93–95 *passim*, 174n7
Everage, Dame Edna (Barry
  Humphries), 158f

Fay, Amy, 61, 64, 76
Fellatio, 9, 173n9
Fétis, François-Joseph, 100
Field, John, 107
Fingering, 24, 40f, 130
Fischer, Bobby, 103
"The Flirtations," 153f
Fontaine, Joan, 85, 87, 89
Foster Jenkins, Florence, 148, 153–54
Foucault, Michel, 75
Friedheim, Arthur, 177n33

Garber, Marjorie, 143, 156, 162, 179n10, 179n13

Gay, Peter, 45

Genet, Jean, 54, 57

Gershwin, George, 142f, 165

Gesticulation, 97, 103, 175n13, 175n14

Gide, André, 7–33 *passim*, 93, 95, 129, 151f, 156, 173n9; *If It Die* (*Si le grain ne meurt*), 9, 28; *The Immoralist*, 27, 31; *Notes on Chopin*, 8–31 *passim*; *Straight Is the Gate*, 25

Gigi (film), 88

Godowsky, Leopold, 14

Gorodnitski, Sascha, 115

Gottschalk, Louis Moreau, 13, 66f, 74, 79, 91, 173n4

Gould, Glenn, 14, 26, 102–5, 107, 112f; vs. Horowitz, 104–5

Graffman, Gary, 128

Grant, Hugh, 94f

Groote, Steven De, 120

Hadow, W. H., 177n31

Hallé, Charles, 97, 175n14

Hansen, Miriam, 180n21

Hanslick, Eduard, 177n32

Hanson, Ellis, 146–47

Haydn, Franz Joseph, 2

Heidegger, Martin, 56

Heine, Heinrich, 97

Hernández, Felisberto, 122–24

Hess, Myra, 117, 136

Hildegarde, 164–65

Holland, Bernard, 104–5

Homophobia, 9, 38–44 *passim*, 55, 62–75 *passim*, 91–107 *passim*, 120–21, 139–58 *passim*

Homosociality, 38–39, 41f, 53, 66, 75, 112, 140, 174n7

Horowitz, Joseph, 109–10, 120–21

Horowitz, Vladimir, 3, 10, 12, 14, 18, 22, 56, 96f, 119, 163; vs. Gould, 104–5; vs. Rubinstein, 96, 105–13 *passim*, 149, 163–64

Horowitz, Wanda, 104f, 112f

Horowitz-Barnay, Ilka, 69–70, 71f, 76ff

Houseman, John, 87f

Hudson, Rock, 143, 153

Hummel, Johann Nepomuk, 68, 76, 174n6

Huneker, James, 66, 74

Impromptu (film), 94–96, 107

Improvisation, 3, 25, 29, 32, 68, 95, 130, 134

Irigaray, Luce, 49

Isherwood, Christopher, 15, 179n11

Iturbi, José, 161, 163

James, Henry, 96, 99, 175n12

Jourdan, Louis, 85–89 *passim*, 142, 162, 167

Juilliard, 3, 60

Kalish, Gilbert, 128

Kalkbrenner, Friedrich, 73, 97

Kaye, Richard, 175n12

Keiler, Allan, 69, 70–76 *passim*, 92, 94, 102, 174n9

Kincaid, James, 74

Klindworth, Karl, 92, 177n32

Koestenbaum, Wayne, 21, 42–46 *passim*, 54f, 59, 85, 117, 119, 136, 154, 156, 173n6

Korsyn, Kevin, 172n5

Kramer, Lawrence, 99, 172n8

Kraus, Lili, 120

Kristeva, Julia, 45, 52

Kuerti, Anton, 102–3, 105

Lateiner, Jacob, 128

Lecuona, Ernesto, 137

Leschetizky, Theodor, 129

Letter from an Unknown Woman (film), 85–89, 91ff, 110, 112, 142, 167, 179n5

Lhevinne, Rosina, 119–20, 136

Liberace, 14, 55, 106, 139–65, 167

Liberation, 23, 95–96, 105, 147, 153
Liebestod, see Romantic love
Lipatti, Dinu, 16, 54, 56
Liszt, Franz, 10, 27, 31, 37–58 *passim*,
61f, 64f, 67–77 *passim*, 79, 81, 85,
89–93 *passim*, 103–20 *passim*, 150,
159, 163, 167; vs. Chopin, 93–100
passim, 108; vs. Thalberg, 97–102
passim
————, works of: *Funérailles*, 13,
37–58 *passim*, 62, 93, 161; *Mazeppa*,
95, 175n9; Sonata in B minor, 108,
177n32, 177n33; *Un Sospiro*, 85, 92,
98, 110, 113, 167; *Waldesrauschen*,
160
Lisztomania (film), 92, 102
Loesser, Arthur, 62–67 *passim*
Lola Montès (film), 86, 92–93
Loudness, 17f, 20–21, 26f, 41–42, 90,
94, 98, 100, 172n8, 174n4
The Loved One (film), 146
Lugosi, Bela, 146

MacLaine, Shirley, 126–27
Madame Sousatzka (film), 126–28
Madonna, 150
"Maiden" piano teachers, 2–3, 98,
106, 109, 113, 115–36, 160
Major and minor, 37, 48, 51, 55, 58,
122, 134
Mann, Thomas, 77–78
Mason & Hamlin, 4, 35
Masturbation, 8f, 13–14, 18, 58, 77f,
89f, 111, 121
Maurice (film), 94
Mendelssohn, Fanny, 100
Mendelssohn, Felix, 1, 100
Middlebrow, 150–60 *passim*, 165,
171n1
Miniaturism, 102, 106f, 109f, 149,
172n8, 176n20, 177n31
"Mister Sandman" (song), 139, 153f,
163
Moon, Michael, 156
Moscheles, Ignaz, 98f, 175n13

Mozart, Wolfgang Amadeus, 5, 24,
51, 71, 108, 154f
Mythic consecrations:
Beethoven/Liszt (*Weihekuss*), 64,
67–78 *passim*, 85, 100, 163; Cho-
pin/Gottschalk, 66–67, 74, 173n4;
Liszt/Tausig, 61–62;
Paderewski/Liberace, 163

Neal, Harry, 128–29
Necrophilia, 40f, 45, 54–56 *passim*,
66, 83, 86
Niceness, 118, 135, 142, 147

Opera queens, 5, 12, 26ff, 43, 101, 108,
133–34, 137, 148, 152
Ophuls, Max, 85f, 88
Orpheus, 53, 130

Paderewski, Ignaz, 91, 139, 147, 155,
162–63, 171n4, 181n24, 181n25,
181n26
Paganini, Niccolò, 76, 100
Parents, 1f, 4, 8, 16, 22ff, 28f, 31, 35, 37,
46–51 *passim*, 53, 62f, 70–73
passim, 79, 83–84, 100, 104, 109,
115, 120, 123, 126f, 132, 139, 142–46
passim, 158–61 *passim*, 174n9,
179n13
Paris Is Burning (film), 153
Parlando, 28–30, 44, 172n7
Patronage, 63f
Pavlova, Anna, 83f
Pederasty, 7–8, 21, 23f, 54, 62–64,
74–75, 77, 79, 113, 163
Perahia, Murray, 176n20
Perényi, Eleanor, 38–40, 65, 69
Performativity, 4, 9f, 30, 85, 118–19,
155–56
Picard, Raymond, 129
Plantinga, Leon, 63–64
Pogorelich, Ivo, 26, 103, 105–6, 177n30
Pollini, Maurizio, 13, 37
Practice, 1, 3, 8f, 12ff, 24–25, 44, 112f,
130, 148, 177n35

Presley, Elvis, 102, 147, 150, 180n14
Programmatic interpretation, 11, 18–20, 37
Proust, Marcel, 7f, 14–15, 105, 129, 152, 156, 171n3
Puccini, Giacomo, 20

Rachmaninov, Sergei, 4, 10, 97; Piano Concerto No. 3, 4, 109–10; Prélude in C-sharp minor, 90f, 107, 174n4, 174n5
Racine, Jean Baptiste, 130
Ramann, Lina, 67–68, 77
Raykoff, Ivan, 154–55
The Red Shoes (film), 84
Richter, Sviatoslav, 22
Romantic love, 4, 9, 19, 45, 47, 57, 77, 90f, 132, 135; crystallization, 4, 53, 124–25, 132; *Liebestod*, 57, 77, 89, 91, 134, 146; Wertherism, 132
Rosen, Charles, 111–12
Rubato, 17, 19–22 *passim*, 25, 29, 149
Rubinstein, Aniela, 112f
Rubinstein, Anton, 107
Rubinstein, Arthur, 10, 14f, 18, 40, 56, 96, 152, 163; vs. Horowitz, 96, 105–13 *passim*, 149, 163–64

Said, Edward, 40, 102, 108
Saint-Saëns, Camille, 4, 83
Sand, George, 39, 93–96 *passim*, 107, 176n19
Sands, Julian, 94
Saphir, Moritz, 97, 106
Satie, Erik, 91, 174n5
Schiff, Andras, 83, 105
Schindler, Anton, 67
Schnabel, Artur, 106f
Schonberg, Harold, 68–69, 106f, 163, 176n21, 176n28, 177n35, 181n26
Schubert, Franz, 53, 96, 119, 171n6; Sonata in B-flat major, 107, 110, 119, 176n28
Schumann, Clara, 29, 40–41, 54, 100, 175n16, 177n32

Schumann, Robert, 8, 10–33 *passim*, 35–53 *passim*, 96–108 *passim*; *Carnaval*, 40f, 175n16; *Fantasie*, 8, 26, 33, 48; *Fröhlicher Landmann*, 59; *Gesänge der Frühe*, 47f; *Kreisleriana*, 18; *Papillons*, 47f; Sonata in F minor, 107; Sonata in F-sharp minor, 108
Schwartzkopf, Elisabeth, 26
Schwarzenegger, Arnold, 42
Scriabin, Alexander, 121f, 176n27
Sedgwick, Eve Kosofsky, 42–46, 49, 54f, 86, 99, 148, 156, 171n3, 173n11
Self-expression, 5, 8, 10–11, 14, 17f, 22, 26, 29–33 *passim*, 48, 96, 102, 118, 123, 133
Seminal economy, 86, 93, 110–13 *passim*, 143, 179n5
Sentimentality, 4, 19–22 *passim*, 42–47 *passim*, 54f, 75, 84, 86, 121–22, 149, 151, 165, 171n3, 173n11
Serkin, Rudolf, 14, 106, 129
Shearer, Moira, 84
Shields, Brooke, 104
Siloti, Alexander, 115
Sincerely Yours (film), 161ff, 167
Slonimsky, Nicolas, 129–30
Smalley, Stuart (Al Franken), 158
Sodomy, 9, 23, 50, 63, 148, 151, 179n9
A Song to Remember (film), 93–94, 95, 100, 161
Speed, 1, 15–17 *passim*, 21f, 25, 35, 90, 94, 130, 151
Stein, Gertrude, 127
Steiner, George, 102f
Steinway & Sons, 35, 127
Stendhal, 53, 126
Stereotypes, 20–28 *passim*, 39f, 44–51 *passim*, 72ff, 102, 107f, 109f, 113, 115, 118, 134, 143–48 *passim*, 158, 173n6, 179n9, 180n18
Stevens, Wallace, 117f
Stoker, Bram, 146
Streisand, Barbra, 26
Suture, 55, 83–91 *passim*

Swann, Jeffrey, 120, 139

Taruskin, Richard, 176n23
Tausig, Carl, 61–62, 76, 79, 97
Tchaikovsky, Peter Ilyitch, 149f; Piano Concerto No. 1, 109, 117, 177n34
Thalberg, Sigismond, 41f, 64ff, 79, 159, 173n3; vs. Liszt, 97–102 *passim*
32 Short Films About Glenn Gould (film), 176n26
Thomas, Marian, 140–42, 151
Thomas, Michael Tilson, 85, 89
Thompson, Michael, 143
Thomson, Virgil, 107
Toradze, Alexander, 120
Toscanini, Arturo, 104
Transcendence, 12, 25, 27, 29, 103, 130
Transcription, 27, 32, 38, 101, 112, 154–55
Transgression, 20f, 23f, 32, 105, 120, 155
Transvestism, 39, 143, 155f, 162, 178n4, 179n10
Trinh Minh-ha, 177n1
Truth, 17, 30f, 46f, 53f, 56–58 *passim*, 77, 92, 113
Twiggy, 126

Valentino, Rudolph, 155, 161f, 180n21
Vampirism, 146f

Vengerova, Isabelle, 128–30
Villoing, Alexander, 107
Virtuosity, 5, 10–33 *passim*, 41, 62, 64f, 76, 83–113, 117–46 *passim*, 161

Wagner, Richard, 20, 96, 134, 146, 150
Wakoski, Diane, 144–46, 151f
Walker, Alan, 38–39, 41, 65f, 69–77 *passim*, 94, 102
Waters, John, 153
Waugh, Evelyn, 179n11
Weihekuss, see Mythic consecrations
Welk, Lawrence, 145
Welles, Orson, 87
Welty, Eudora, 130–33, 135–36, 160
West, Mae, 155–57 *passim*, 180n21
Wharton, Edith, 96, 175n12
What Ever Happened to Baby Jane? (film), 84
Wieck, Friedrich, 100, 102
Wilde, Cornel, 93, 161f
Wilde, Oscar, 14, 30f, 49, 53, 89–91 *passim*, 132, 139, 150–56 *passim*, 179n7, 180n18
Without You I'm Nothing (film), 153
Woolf, Virginia, 51–54 *passim*

Yingling, Thomas, 180n18

Zweig, Stefan, 86–87

Library of Congress Cataloging-in-Publication Data

Kopelson, Kevin.
   Beethoven's Kiss : pianism, perversion, and the
   mastery of desire / Kevin Kopelson
         p.   cm.
   Includes bibliographical references and index.
   ISBN 0-8047-2597-7 (cloth : alk. paper). —
   ISBN 0-8047-2598-5 (pbk. : alk. paper)
   1. Piano music—19th century—History and
   criticism.   2. Piano music—20th century—
   History and criticism.   3. Pianists—Sexual
   behavior.   4. Sexuality in music.   I. Title.
   ML700.K56   1996
   786.2'08'664—dc20   95-23459
                                               CIP
                                               MN

   ⊚   This book is printed on acid-free recycled paper.

Original printing 1996
Last figure below indicates year of this printing

05   04   03   02   01   00   99   98   97   96